KEYS TO
Successful
LIVING

Other Books by Derek Prince

KEYS TO
Successful
LIVING

12 WAYS TO DISCOVER
GOD'S BEST FOR YOUR LIFE

DEREK PRINCE

Chosen
a division of Baker Publishing Group
Minneapolis, Minnesota

© 2014 by Derek Prince Ministries International

Published by Chosen Books
11400 Hampshire Avenue South
Bloomington, Minnesota 55438
www.chosenbooks.com

Chosen Books is a division of
Baker Publishing Group, Grand Rapids, Michigan

Printed in the United States of America

Library of Congress Cataloging-in-Publication Data is on file Library of Congress in Washington DC.

ISBN 978-0-8007-9618-1 (pbk.)

Unless otherwise indicated, Scripture quotations are from the New American Standard Bible®, copyright © 1960, 1962, 1963, 1968, 1971, 1972, 1973 by The Lockman Foundation. Used by permission.

Scripture identified NIV1984 taken from the HOLY BIBLE, NEW INTERNATIONAL VERSION®. Copyright © 1973, 1978, 1984 Biblica. Used by permission of Zondervan. All rights reserved.

Scripture quotations identified NKJV are from the New King James Version. Copyright © 1982 by Thomas Nelson, Inc. Used by permission. All rights reserved.

This book was compiled from the extensive archives of Derek Prince's unpublished materials, and edited by the Derek Prince Ministries editorial team.

Cover design by Dual Identity

14   15   16   17   18   19   20   7   6   5   4   3   2   1

Contents

Preface

Is LIFE GOING WELL FOR YOU? *Would you consider your life a success?*

If you answer yes to these two questions, you will probably enjoy this book by Derek Prince. Very likely, it will confirm some of the principles you are already applying to make your life successful.

On the other hand, if you answer no to the two questions above, you will probably enjoy this book by Derek Prince. In fact, it may provide a life-altering pathway, making all the difference in how the rest of your life works out for you.

Over the years, maybe you have read a number of self-help books designed to bring you success. Maybe the results you have experienced have been mixed at best. We believe you will find a refreshingly practical approach in *Keys to*

Successful Living. If you have been looking for keys, you just found twelve powerful ones in this book.

Biblical/Practical

During his sixty years of teaching ministry, Derek Prince (1915–2003) made a number of agreements with the Lord. One of them was a promise that he would not simply present nice religious lectures. Rather, he would always give people an opportunity to respond to the Word of God each time he taught. When Derek originally presented this material as a series of fifteen-minute broadcasts on his popular radio program, also called *Keys to Successful Living,* those responses from listeners started to occur. And they haven't stopped yet.

The original title of the radio series was *Twelve Steps to a Good Year,* referring to twelve purposeful statements found in the book of Hebrews. Derek knew that these twelve steps, systematically applied in the lives of those who put them into practice, would serve as a catalyst for change. We are talking about *life* change here.

The response to Derek's teaching from every audience who has heard it has been so positive that this radio series is still regularly featured around the beginning of the year—a time when all of us reevaluate our lives and make some deliberate decisions. But as chapter 1 so clearly states, this is not just a New Year's resolution book. It has the potential to help you any time you need a new start. The steps Derek highlights in this book represent that wonderful combination of biblical truth and practical action that can transform any life at any time—yours included.

We pray that as you apply these twelve resolutions from the book of Hebrews, you will find them to be powerful keys that unlock the life God intends for you to be living.

What This Book Can Do for You

Many of Derek Prince's books have become foundational manuals on a variety of subjects: fasting, spiritual warfare, the new birth, baptism, the power of the Holy Spirit, etc. (See the list on page 2 of this book for specific titles of Derek's works published on these topics.) These foundational, "go-to" books are absorbed and reread time and again. We think the same phenomenon will apply to *Keys to Successful Living*.

The steps outlined in this book are not "mandates"—they are more like platforms on which you can stand and progressively build. Why not take the time to read through this book without rushing? As you do, prayerfully consider which resolution you would like to start with. You do not have to start with Key #1, and you don't have to start on January 1. Pick the key or keys that resonate with you right now. It is up to you.

If you have never had much previous success with attempts at new starts in life, you may be wondering if you should make any attempt at all. You might be tempted to think, "I'd be happy to get just *one* of these resolutions under my belt." That might be true.

But before you throw in the towel, here are two interesting statistics from a university study. First statistic: *Only 8 percent of those who make New Year's resolutions succeed.* (Okay, that is not very encouraging . . . but keep reading.) Here is the second statistic: *The people who explicitly make resolutions are ten times more likely to attain their goals than people who do not explicitly make resolutions.*[1] Even if you succeed with only one, you have already made progress *just by trying!* Even by picking up this book and holding it in your hand, you are taking a step.

Are you ready for a new start? Are you ready to move ahead to apply twelve powerful decisions from the book of Hebrews that have the potential to change your life forever?

Then let's get started.

The International Editorial Team
of Derek Prince Ministries

---

1. University of Scranton, "New Year's Resolution Statistics," *Journal of Clinical Psychology*, January 1, 2014, www.statisticbrain.com/new-years-resolution-statistics.

1

Right Resolutions

CAN WE MAKE DELIBERATE Bible-inspired decisions that will cause us to experience a higher quality of life? The answer is a resounding yes! That is the message of this book.

This theme is especially designed to equip you with an attitude and an outlook to help you appropriate the fullness of God's provision for you. It will open the way to God's blessings for the rest of your life, beginning with the months that lie just ahead. You see, so much depends on these two factors—your attitude and your outlook—as you move into all God has planned for you.

Why Make Resolutions?

If you think about this from the perspective of beginning a new year—traditionally associated with making resolutions—then you will see what I mean. When I was a boy growing up, making resolutions was a common practice (though it may not be quite so fashionable today). At the end of the old year, most people would decide to make good changes in their lives for the coming new year. At the same time, they would usually be laughing at themselves, knowing all too well that their resolutions would not last very long. Even so, I do believe that on a regular basis (whether in January of each new year or any other time) it is appropriate to make resolutions or to reaffirm those that were previously made.

You see, resolutions determine our attitude. Our attitude, in turn, determines our approach to any situation. And our approach to any situation determines the outcome. Let me restate that sequence:

Resolutions determine attitude.

Attitude determines approach.

Approach determines the outcome.

The way you approach a new year (wherever that falls on the calendar) will ultimately determine the outcome of that year in your life. A wrong approach will lead to an unfavorable outcome. A right approach in response to God will lead to a successful outcome. Your approach is decisive. And your approach depends ultimately on the resolutions you choose to follow.

Twelve "Let Us" Keys

The New Testament book of Hebrews provides us with important statements that can show us the way to successful outcomes, no matter what situations we are facing. They stand out because each is introduced by the phrase *Let us*. I have gone carefully through this letter to Hebrew believers in the original language (which is Greek), and I have discovered there are precisely twelve such *Let us* sentences found there. These *Let us* sentences constitute twelve good resolutions—or, as I prefer to call them, "Twelve Keys to a Successful Year." We could broaden that to say: "Twelve Keys to a Successful Life."

These keys are listed below in the order in which they occur in the epistle to the Hebrews. This will give you an overall view of the material we will cover in this book. (The first one is surprising. You probably would never have guessed it, and you might be surprised by how we develop it later.)

Key #1: Let us fear

Key #2: Let us be diligent

Key #3: Let us hold fast our confession

Key #4: Let us draw near to the throne of grace

Key #5: Let us press on to maturity

Key #6: Let us draw near to the Most Holy Place

Key #7: Let us hold fast our confession without wavering

Key #8: Let us consider one another

Key #9: Let us run with endurance the race set before us

Key #10: Let us show gratitude

Key #11: Let us go out to Him

Key #12: Let us offer up a sacrifice of praise

There are a couple of interesting points in this list. Two of these keys begin with *Let us draw near*. The first one says, "Let us draw near to the throne of grace"; the second says, "Let us draw near to the Most Holy Place." Also, you will notice that *Let us hold fast our confession* occurs twice. But the second time, a significant phrase is added: "Let us hold fast our confession *without wavering*." We will look at these and many other specific points in the chapters that follow.

"Let Us . . ."

I want to dwell for a moment here on the significance of the phrase used at the beginning of each key: *Let us*. This phrase gives us two specific concepts. First of all, it denotes a resolution, as I have already stated. Second, we take note that the resolution is in the plural. It is never "Let me" or "I will." It is always "Let us."

This indicates not merely that we need to make certain resolutions, but also that we have the most benefit when believers make them together. I think that the Holy Spirit is emphasizing this in a special way to God's people at this time in world history. We are not independent, autonomous units—each of us making it through life on his or her own, regardless of our fellow believers. To the contrary—in a very real sense, we are dependent on one another. If we are going to make it through to the fulfillment of God's purposes, we are going to have to do it together. We will never do it separately as individuals.

In Ephesians 4, Paul is talking about the ministries that the Lord has set in His Church for various basic purposes, such as the building up of the Body of Christ, the maturing (or perfecting) of the saints, and so on. In verse 13, Paul sums up the purposes of these ministries: "Until we all reach unity in the faith and in the knowledge of the Son of God and become mature, attaining to the whole measure of the fullness of Christ" (NIV1984).

In the same connection, with reference to Jesus Christ, Paul says in verse 16: "From him [Christ] the whole body, joined and held together by every supporting ligament, grows and builds itself up in love, as each part does its work" (NIV1984).

Please notice that the emphasis in both those verses is on the collective rather than the individual. Speaking about unity, the full knowledge of the Son of God, and maturity, Paul uses the words *we all*: "Until *we all* reach unity in the faith and in the knowledge of the Son of God. Until *we all* become mature. Until *we all* attain to the whole measure of the fullness of Christ." The implication is clear: We are not going to do this on our own; we are dependent upon our fellow believers. Thus, the resolutions we make are not just individualistic, self-centered steps concerning what *I am* going to do this year. Instead, they are decisions that affect our fellow believers: *Let us.*

We see this principle clearly in the sixteenth verse, where Paul points out how much we are dependent upon one another. The "whole body" is a unit, joined together by "every supporting ligament." It only "grows and builds itself up in love, as each part does its work."

In the natural human body, if one part malfunctions it almost inevitably affects other parts. If, for instance, the liver fails, other main areas and systems of the human body will fail as well. All those other areas and systems, therefore, are dependent on the liver. In the same way, we as Christians are dependent upon one another. We will talk further, in chapters 5 and 8, about these keys as they relate to the body of believers.

I will go through each of the twelve keys to successful living in detail in chapters 3 through 14, articulating how each one applies to you—and, therefore, to any situation you are facing. These keys will open the way for you to experience a good year—and a good life. As we embrace these keys to successful living, all of us as believers can grow into fullness, strengthening ourselves and one another.

2

The Background of Hebrews

IN COVERING THIS very important topic of godly intentions and the keys that help us succeed, let us look first at the background of the Hebrew believers to whom these encouragements were written. I believe that an understanding of the culture of these believers provides some lessons for us as Christians today. Then we will explore each of the keys in the chapters that follow.

In many respects, we have inherited the special privileges that were enjoyed by the early Hebrew believers. But we have also inherited the special problems that go with those privileges. You see, the Hebrews, as the very name indicates, had a different background from all other New Testament believers. All of the other epistles (perhaps with the exception of those of James and Peter) were addressed to believers who had come from non-Jewish backgrounds. In other words, they were written to Gentile believers. But the epistle to the Hebrews was specifically and primarily addressed to believers from a Jewish background. That Jewish background gave them many advantages—many special privileges—that were not enjoyed by the Gentiles or the pagans from other nations and backgrounds.

Three Advantages

What were some of these advantages? First of all, these Jewish believers had been freed for many centuries from the awful iniquities of idolatry and false cults. The Law of Moses, by which they ordered their lives, abounds with warnings against these two practices, which are both abominations in God's sight.

In addition, they had a thorough knowledge of the Old Testament Scriptures—the special, unique revelation God gave through His Word in the Old Testament to the Jewish people.

And finally, Jews had familiarity with the Temple, its sacrifices, the forms of worship and the beautiful liturgies. These represented many advantages that could have strengthened and purified their faith. But the sad truth is that many of these Jewish believers had not made proper use of these benefits.

That is why the writer of the letter had to bring some sad and solemn words to them:

> We have much to say about this, but it is hard to explain because you are slow to learn. In fact, though by this time you ought to be teachers, you need someone to teach you the elementary truths of God's word all over again. You need milk, not solid food! Anyone who lives on milk, being still an infant, is not acquainted with the teaching about righteousness. But solid food is for the mature, who by constant use have trained themselves to distinguish good from evil.
>
> Hebrews 5:11–14 NIV1984

Is that not a tragic condition to be in? To be slow to learn, when you have that special background? The condition described in these verses is what I call "the tragedy of arrested spiritual development." These people should have been mature grown-ups. Instead, they were still spiritual infants, not able to take more than milk. I believe the same is true of many, many professing Christians in our world today.

The Hebrews were in that condition because they had failed to do what the writer said. They had not, by constant use, trained themselves to distinguish good from evil. They had not applied themselves to the study of Scripture. They had not given sufficient priority to spiritual pursuits in their lives. As a result of this condition, the epistle to the Hebrews contains more solemn warnings of the danger of falling away than any other book in the New Testament. That in itself is a remarkable fact.

Warnings about Falling Away

Here are five brief quotations from five different passages in Hebrews that contain these solemn warnings.

> We must pay more careful attention, therefore, to what we have heard, so that we do not drift away. For if the message spoken by angels was binding, and every violation and disobedience received its just punishment, how shall we escape if we ignore such a great salvation?
>
> Hebrews 2:1–3 NIV1984

The two dangers cited there are *drifting* and *ignoring*. The second warning is found in Hebrews 3:

> See to it, brothers, that none of you has a sinful, unbelieving heart that turns away from the living God.
>
> Hebrews 3:12 NIV1984

The great danger here is *unbelief*. Next, we see the third warning:

> We do not want you to become lazy, but to imitate those who through faith and patience inherit what has been promised.
>
> Hebrews 6:12 NIV1984

The danger here is *laziness*—spiritual laziness. Here is the fourth warning:

So do not throw away your confidence; it will be richly rewarded. You need to persevere so that when you have done the will of God, you will receive what he has promised.

Hebrews 10:35–36 NIV1984

The danger here is *failing to persevere*—not holding on. Finally, the fifth warning:

See to it that you do not refuse him who speaks. If they did not escape when they refused him who warned them on earth, how much less will we, if we turn away from him who warns us from heaven?

Hebrews 12:25 NIV1984

The danger here is *refusing to hear God when He speaks*. It is truly remarkable that people who had inherited spiritual privileges had to be warned of these terrible dangers.

Today's Christians

Through these verses, we see the condition of the Hebrew Christians—the Jewish believers—at the beginning of the New Testament age more than two thousand years ago. Today, in a certain sense, the shoe is on the other foot. It is not primarily Jewish believers who are in danger, but believers from non-Jewish backgrounds—people from so-called Christian nations. These are people who have been "born" in the Christian church. They are people who automatically call themselves Christians without ever stopping to consider what that means.

Look at the fact that many professing Christians today enjoy the same kind of privileges that the early Hebrew Christians enjoyed. First, they have been delivered from idolatry. Well, that is true of multitudes of professing Christians. They have no thought of deliberate idolatry.

Second, the Hebrews had knowledge of the Scriptures. That is also true, to a degree, of many professing Christians today. In some measure, they know the Scriptures—the Old Testament and the New.

Third, the Hebrews were familiar with the services at the Temple. I find many, many Christians who are in some measure familiar with church services, religious terminology, forms of prayer, and ceremonies—all of which probably contain within them some tremendous gems of spiritual truth.

Yet it is a sad fact, using a well-known phrase, that many times "familiarity breeds contempt." We become so used to certain practices that we take them for granted. We fail to appreciate what is available to us. This means that we need the same warnings the Hebrews received—warnings against drifting, being negligent, being lazy, presuming on God's grace and taking privileges for granted that are extremely precious and important.

This description in Hebrews looks strikingly like multitudes of professing Christians. Could it possibly be a picture of you? If that is the case, I would suggest to you that the remedy is just the same as it was for the Hebrew Christians.

That is exactly why—in the epistle—we have the phrase *Let us* twelve times.

Those twelve *Let us* phrases address the spiritual condition that was the particular problem of the Hebrew Christians—which, almost by inheritance, is the particular problem of multitudes of professing Christians today, especially in Western cultures.

With that sober warning ringing in our ears, then, we turn our attention to each of the *Let us* statements in Hebrews. I believe that these twelve keys can open the way to the successful future God has planned for you. Let's get started.

3

Let Us Fear

LET US. These words indicate resolution—individual decision—as well as steps we take with our fellow believers. Taken together, these *Let us* statements give us twelve keys that open the doors to success in all that we do. Let's begin, then, with the first key.

If we did not understand the spiritual condition of the Hebrew believers to whom this letter was written, which I covered in the last chapter, this first key could really take us aback. But in the light of that background, we can see that it is appropriate—in fact, absolutely necessary.

KEY #1

"Let us fear"

Therefore, let us fear lest, while a promise remains of entering [God's] rest, any one of you should seem to have come short of it.

Hebrews 4:1

Can you see why the first key is "Let us fear"? It is because of the presumption of the Hebrew believers—because of their false security, because of their laziness, because they had not availed themselves of all the privileges and blessings offered to them.

The writer to the Hebrews also gives them a specific example of why they should fear. This example is taken from the past history of the people of Israel. It is based on the experience of the Israelites in their journey through the wilderness from Egypt to the Promised Land—and what God said to them during that journey. The quotation is actually from one of the psalms. It is what God said to Israel in connection with their attitude and their conduct in their time of wilderness wandering.

So, as the Holy Spirit says: "Today, if you hear his voice, do not harden your hearts as you did in the rebellion, during the time of testing in the desert [or wilderness], where your fathers tested and tried me and for forty years saw what I did. That is

why I was angry with that generation, and I said, 'Their hearts
are always going astray, and they have not known my ways.'"

Hebrews 3:7–10 NIV1984

What we read here is a remarkable fact. God brought that
whole generation out of Egypt by many miraculous wonders;
nevertheless, because of their subsequent conduct, He was
angry with them. Then the Scripture goes on—and this is
God speaking: "So I declared on oath in my anger, 'They shall
never enter my rest'" (verse 11 NIV1984).

Immediately following that statement by the Lord, we see
the application in the admonition given:

> See to it, brothers, that none of you has a sinful, unbelieving
> heart that turns away from the living God. But encourage
> one another daily, as long as it is called Today, so that none
> of you may be hardened by sin's deceitfulness. We have come
> to share in Christ if we hold firmly till the end the confidence
> we had at first. As has just been said: "Today, if you hear his
> voice, do not harden your hearts as you did in the rebellion."

> verses 12–15 NIV1984

The essence of this warning is: "Do not harden your hearts."

Hear God's Voice

In what, exactly, did Israel's generation fail? I think the above
passage makes it clear. There was one basic failure—they

did not hear God's voice. They were content to get things secondhand through Moses.

Those Israelites, who so angered God, had only a form of religion. They had the Tabernacle, the Ten Commandments, the priesthood, the sacrifices and the various laws of ceremonial cleanliness. But in all that, they missed the one essential. They were so satisfied with externals that they missed the one pursuit that could have saved them from disaster. The one factor that could have carried them through to God's rest for them.

What was that? They failed to hear God's voice.

Lest we think that we are removed from their experience, look again at the first key: "Let *us* fear." In other words, this injunction is not restricted to the Israelites in the wilderness. The Israelites are merely put forward as an example and a warning to us. That warning applies still to us today. "Let us fear."

How do we accomplish this? We stay very much on our guard; we are careful not to make the same mistake the Israelites made in the wilderness. Their mistake was to focus on externals and, thus, miss the real, inner, essential practice of hearing God's voice.

The principle illustrated by this warning runs all through the Bible. The one basic essential for a right relationship with God is to hear His voice. Jesus says the same to us as His disciples in the New Testament: "My sheep hear My voice, and I know them, and they follow Me" (John 10:27).

I believe that is perhaps the clearest and simplest description of true Christians found anywhere in the New Testament.

When Jesus says *My sheep*, He is speaking about those who truly believe in Him, those whom He acknowledges and accepts—being Himself the Good Shepherd. He makes two very simple statements about them. First, "My sheep hear My voice." Second, "They follow Me."

Do We Hear His Voice?

That is true of all real Christians. They hear the Lord's voice and they follow Him. It is not possible to follow the Lord if you do not hear His voice. The pattern Jesus gives of the ancient shepherd and his sheep is clear: The sheep follow the shepherd because they hear his voice. If they did not hear his voice, they could not follow him.

The essential element, then, is to hear the voice of Jesus and to follow Him. Stating it another way, the danger is making the same mistake the Israelites made in the wilderness. What was that error? Becoming preoccupied with externals—with religion, ceremonies and laws—but missing that basic, inner, essential component: hearing the voice of the Lord.

I urge you today to consider the importance of learning to hear the Lord's voice. This does not mean that you learn a set of religious rules. It does not even mean that you read your Bible every day, though that is good. Nor does it mean that you say your prayers every day, though that also is good. Hearing the voice of the Lord means having that intimate, personal relationship with the Lord where He can speak to you directly and personally, whether through the Bible or some other way.

Jesus never said, "My sheep read the Bible." It is a good habit to read the Bible *if* you hear the Lord's voice. But many people read the Bible without hearing the Lord's voice. They miss the essential factor.

I want to make this promise to you: If you will begin using this first key, you will be a better person by the time you have learned how to use all twelve of them. Let us fear making the same mistake Israel made. Let us cultivate the practice of hearing the Lord's voice.

4

Let Us Be Diligent

WERE YOU STARTLED by the first resolution? We found it in Hebrews 4:1: "Let us fear." That is not the kind of step most of us would take unless we were directed to do so by the Word of God. Remember that this was particularly appropriate because of the spiritual condition of the Hebrew believers. What was that condition? *Presumption, carelessness, laziness*—a general failure to benefit from all the special spiritual blessings they enjoyed. They seemed to be taking it for granted that they were God's people. In that position, they probably felt rather superior to others—and that they were not required to do much to maintain that superiority.

In essence, they had stopped listening for His voice. Thus, the first key to any measure of true success reminded them to fear the loss of what was most essential in their lives. This was appropriate to Hebrew believers in those days—and to us, professing Christians who are, for the most part, not of Jewish origin.

Let's look now at the next scriptural key to a life of blessing. The second *Let us* resolution occurs later in the fourth chapter of Hebrews.

KEY #2

"Let us be diligent"

Let us therefore be diligent to enter that rest, lest anyone fall through following the same example of disobedience.

Hebrews 4:11

This second key is based on the experience of the Israelites when they were on their journey from Egypt through the wilderness. Many of them never made it through to the promised destination—the rest God had promised them—because of their misconduct and their wrong attitude; consequently, they died in the wilderness. Scripture testifies that their corpses fell in the wilderness because of unbelief and disobedience (see Numbers 14:29, 33). Once again, they had the externals, but they did not have the great, essential, inner reality of true religion—hearing the voice of the Lord.

We see that this mistake of Israel was a tragic error. After pointing out the flawed example of their forefathers—the failure to hear God's voice—the writer of Hebrews goes on to say, "Let us be diligent." I believe what he describes with that second key is a natural progression. If we really take to heart the dangers of the Israelites' spiritual condition—and we respond properly with a sense of godly fear—the next step we will naturally take is to become diligent.

What Is Diligence?

Let's consider for a moment what diligence is. Sometimes one way to find out the meaning of a word is to consider its opposite. One obvious opposite of *diligence* is *laziness*.

The Bible has not one good word to say about laziness. Actually, this theme does not receive enough attention in contemporary Christendom. Look, for instance, at what the writer of Hebrews says about it:

> We want each of you to show this same diligence to the very end, in order to make your hope sure. We do not want you to become lazy, but to imitate those who through faith and patience inherit what has been promised.

> Hebrews 6:11–12 NIV1984

The warning here is that we need to be not only diligent, but diligent to the very end. We must continue to be diligent. The opposite of *diligence* is there stated in plain words—it is to become lazy. This is not primarily a physical laziness, but spiritual laziness.

Let's compare what we have seen so far with the words of Peter. In his second epistle, he says this:

> For this very reason, make every effort ["applying all diligence" NASB] to add to your faith goodness; and to goodness, knowledge; and to knowledge, self-control; and to self-control, perseverance; and to perseverance, godliness; and to godliness, brotherly kindness; and to brotherly kindness, love.
>
> 2 Peter 1:5–7 NIV1984

You see, the Christian life is not a static condition. Rather, it is a life of adding. It is a life of growth and of progress. To be static in the Christian life is to backslide. But to move forward and do that adding requires diligence. It requires making every effort. In this same passage Peter goes on with an *if*.

> For if you possess these qualities in increasing measure, they will keep you from being ineffective and unproductive in your knowledge of our Lord Jesus Christ. But if anyone does not have them, he is nearsighted and blind, and has forgotten that he has been cleansed from his past sins.
>
> 2 Peter 1:8–9 NIV1984

Do you believe that the condition Peter describes could be possible? That somebody who has been cleansed from past sins could possibly forget that it has even happened? It may seem implausible to you, but Scripture indicates it is possible.

Peter really sets before us two alternatives. The one is to be effective and productive in our knowledge of the Lord Jesus Christ. The other is to be ineffective and unproductive with a condition he describes as being "nearsighted and blind." I think you would agree that those are strong words.

In light of this potential in each of us, Peter continues in the next two verses:

> Therefore, my brothers [because of the warning Peter has given], be all the more eager to make your calling and election sure. For if you do these things, you will never fall, and you will receive a rich welcome into the eternal kingdom of our Lord and Savior Jesus Christ.
>
> 2 Peter 1:10–11 NIV1984

What Peter says here is really good news. There are actions we can take to guarantee that we will never fall. Actions that will guarantee that we will have a rich welcome into the Kingdom of our Lord.

We see from these passages that, basically, the condition we are warned against is laziness. I am deeply troubled about the lack of concern in Christian circles about laziness. The majority of Christians, for instance, view sins like drunkenness with horror. But in the Scriptures, laziness is much more severely condemned than drunkenness. The problem is that many Christians who would never be found in a drunken state are habitually lazy. What is our conclusion? Let's use that second key and be diligent.

Making Diligence Practical

Consider for a moment some additional aspects of what is involved in diligence. Two beautiful verses in Proverbs 10 have long been a kind of guiding light to me in my own experience. Together they sum up the two conditions for true riches or enduring wealth. One condition is on the Lord's side; the other condition is on our side. Both conditions must be fulfilled to attain the result.

Here is the condition on the Lord's side: "It is the blessing of the LORD that makes rich, and He adds no sorrow to it" (Proverbs 10:22). Clearly, the great, primary condition for true riches, spiritual and otherwise, is the blessing of the Lord. We cannot count on anything really good apart from the blessing of the Lord.

On the other hand, the blessing of the Lord, by itself, is not sufficient. Proverbs 10:4 gives us our side of the equation: "Poor is he who works with a negligent hand, but the hand of the diligent makes rich."

First of all, the blessing of the Lord makes rich. But second of all, the hand of the diligent makes rich. It takes the Lord's blessing plus our diligence to attain to true wealth. It is not enough simply to expect the blessing of the Lord or even to receive the blessing of the Lord. It will not accomplish its purpose in your life unless you add to it your own personal diligence. (Remember, diligence is the opposite of laziness.)

Here is my testimony: I have proved these two Scriptures true in my own experience through many years of Christian living. I have been in many different situations, in many different forms of ministry, in many different lands and on different continents. By the grace of God, I can testify that I have always displayed diligence in small things and in great things. In every situation for which I have had to shoulder responsibilities, I have left that situation in a better condition—spiritually, financially, in every obvious way—than it was when I found it.

First and foremost, I thank the Lord for His blessing. But the blessing of the Lord would never have been fully realized had I not added to it my own diligence. As we close this chapter, let me leave those two words with you: "The blessing of the Lord makes rich," but also "the hand of the diligent makes rich." Add those two together and you have true spiritual riches. What is the underlying factor for all of this? It is our second key from Hebrews: "Let us be diligent."

5

Let Us Hold Fast Our Confession

As we observed earlier, this book's special purpose is to
equip you with a good attitude and outlook. You can use the
twelve keys given here to help you appropriate the fullness of
God's provision and His blessing in the days ahead. I suggest,
therefore, that you make a point to memorize them. Then, by
the time you finish this book, you will have more than just
a general impression; you will have positive and permanent
steps to take with you into the future.

To help you in this, I will list the keys at the opening of
each chapter as we go along. Here again are the first two:

1. Let us fear
2. Let us be diligent

In this chapter, we go on to the third key—the third *Let us* found in the book of Hebrews. This one, like the first two, is found in the fourth chapter (actually, the first four keys are all found in Hebrews 4). It has to do with the words that come out of our mouths.

KEY #3

"Let us hold fast our confession"

Since then we have a great high priest who has passed through the heavens, Jesus the Son of God, let us hold fast our confession.

Hebrews 4:14

The word *confession* is derived from a word in the original Greek of the New Testament that means "to say the same as." The basic meaning of *confession*, therefore, is "saying the same as." In its scriptural context, *confession* means that we say the same as God says. We make the words of our mouths agree with God's Word.

There is a further implication in the word *confession*. It means that we "say it out boldly"—that we are not intimidated. The word *confession* has a considerable history in the foundations of the Christian Church. Certain "confessions," or statements of faith, have been significant for God's people throughout the ages. In many eras, it has taken boldness and courage on the part of those who made these confessions to take the stand they took. But the Bible encourages us in this regard: "Let us hold fast our confession."

Jesus as High Priest and Advocate

In the context of this third *Let us* statement, the writer of Hebrews then points out particularly the confession that relates us to Jesus as our High Priest. Many Christians do not have a clear picture of Jesus as High Priest, yet it is one of His most important ongoing ministries on our behalf. Jesus is there as our representative in the presence of God the Father, standing as guarantor for us. Every time we make the right confession—we say the right, positive declaration with our mouths—Jesus has obligated Himself to ensure that our confession is made good in our experience.

Here is what the writer of Hebrews says just a little earlier in chapter 3: "Therefore, holy brethren, partakers of a heavenly calling, consider Jesus, the Apostle and High Priest of our confession" (Hebrews 3:1).

Notice those last words, "[the] High Priest of our confession." That means that our confession enlists Jesus as our High Priest. Unfortunately, the opposite is also true. If we do not make a confession, we have no High Priest. Not that Jesus has ceased to be our High Priest, but we have given Him no opportunity to minister as such.

Jesus is the High Priest of *our confession*. If we make the right proclamations in faith, with our mouths, according to Scripture, then Jesus has eternally obligated Himself to see that we will never be put to shame—we will always come into the experience of what we confess. However, if we fail to make the right declaration, then, alas, we silence the lips of our High Priest. Lacking our confession, He has nothing to say on our behalf for us in heaven.

In connection with this, Jesus in 1 John 2:1 is also called our Advocate. The word *advocate* is pretty similar to the modern word *attorney*. Jesus is the legal expert who is there to plead our case in heaven. He has never lost a case. But if we do not make a confession, He has no case to plead. So the case goes against us by default.

The Relation to Salvation

Can you see how important confession is? It is vitally important that we give heed to this third *Let us* of Hebrews: "Let us hold fast our confession." This principle of right confession—saying the right words with our mouths—has a central place in the Gospel and in our experience of salvation. In fact, there is no salvation without right confession. Here is what Paul says in Romans 10, in which he explains as clearly as anywhere in the New Testament what is required for salvation. He begins this way:

> "The word is near you, in your mouth and in your heart"—
> that is, the word of faith which we are preaching [The basis
> for salvation is the word. It has to be appropriated by faith.
> This is the message:], that if you confess with your mouth
> Jesus as Lord, and believe in your heart that God raised
> Him from the dead, you shall be saved.
>
> Romans 10:8–9

There are two steps we have to take: one with the heart, one with the mouth. First, we have to believe with the heart. But next, we have to confess, or say it out, with the mouth.

In the next verse, Paul explains further: "for with the heart man believes, resulting in righteousness, and with the mouth he confesses, resulting in salvation" (Romans 10:10).

We see from this a vital principle: no confession, no salvation. It is good to believe in your heart, but that is not sufficient. Not only must you believe in your heart—you must also say it out boldly with your mouth, making the words of your mouth agree with the Word of God.

Confession Determines Destiny

Our initial confession relates us to Jesus as our High Priest. His ongoing ministry on our behalf as High Priest, however, depends on our ongoing confession. The whole Bible shows that our words determine our destiny. Would you like to see a penetrating Scripture that makes this point? Here is one: "Death and life are in the power of the tongue, and those who love it will eat its fruit" (Proverbs 18:21).

We will have one of two results in our lives: Either the tongue is going to produce death if we make a wrong confession, or it is going to produce life if we make a right confession. Scripture attests that we are going to eat the fruit of whatever we say with our tongues.

Look at the words of Jesus: "And I say to you, that every careless word that men shall speak, they shall render account for it in the day of judgment. For by your words you shall be justified, and by your words you shall be condemned" (Matthew 12:36–37).

I have often heard Christians make silly statements they really do not mean—ones that are not honoring to God. Then they excuse themselves by saying, "Well, I didn't really mean it!" But Jesus says, "Every careless word that people speak, they shall give an account for it in the day of judgment." It is not an excuse to say you did not mean it. You must hold fast your confession.

Two Alternatives

Ultimately, we only have two alternatives in our relationship to Christ and to Scripture: to confess or to deny. Listen to what Jesus says:

"Every one therefore who shall confess Me before men, I will also confess him before My Father who is in heaven. [That is His response as our High Priest. If we confess Him, He confesses us. But the alternative is given in the next verse:] But whoever shall deny Me before men, I will also deny him before My Father who is in heaven."

Matthew 10:32–33

Beyond those two choices, ultimately, there is no third alternative. In the long run, with spiritual matters there is no neutrality. Jesus said, "He who is not with Me is against Me" (Matthew 12:30). Either you are going to make the right confession to salvation, or you are going to make a wrong confession, and it will not produce salvation.

"Let us hold fast our confession." Keep affirming your faith verbally. Use the positive to exclude the negative.

6

Let Us Draw Near to the Throne of Grace

As WE MAKE RIGHT CONFESSIONS, we find that we grow in confidence. This is exactly how the Father wants us to come to Him; He will respond to the words of our right confessions, pouring out His blessings and provisions.

Here are the first three keys we have covered so far:

1. Let us fear
2. Let us be diligent
3. Let us hold fast our confession

Now we are moving on to the fourth key, which is also found in Hebrews 4.

KEY #4

"Let us draw near to the throne of grace"

Let us therefore draw near with confidence to the throne of grace, that we may receive mercy and may find grace to help in time of need.

Hebrews 4:16

This fourth key is directly related to the first three, and there is significance in the sequence. In order to be able to draw near with confidence to the throne of grace, we need to make sure we have taken the first three steps.

Let us fear. We should come with an attitude of reverence and awareness of our need of God's grace.

Let us be diligent. This is our response to God's grace. We are not slack, nor lazy, nor indifferent, nor presumptuous. We recognize that God's grace is no excuse for our indifference or presumption. Rather, it should provoke us to be diligent.

Let us hold fast our confession. I believe we must have the right confession. We have to say with our mouths the right statements about Jesus and what He has done for us if we are going to be able to use that fourth key of approaching the throne of grace with confidence.

Mercy and Grace

In regard to our approaching the throne of grace, we are told to come for two benefits: mercy and grace. It is my conviction that if God in His Word invites us to come, and if we meet the conditions that I have briefly outlined, we can come. And if God says that mercy and grace are waiting for us, then I believe we can count on mercy and grace. We need never be disappointed. God will never give us an invitation that He would not stand behind.

Many of the promises and invitations in the Bible are conditional. God says, "If you will do this and this, I'll do that." In this instance, I believe God is saying to us, "If you will approach My throne, having met the conditions, and if you will acknowledge your need of My mercy and My grace, then you can count on it. I will make My mercy and My grace available to you." We do not need to be in any doubt about the truth of this promise from God.

That is the very reason why I believe Scripture says, "Let us draw near *with confidence* to the throne of grace." If we come as God's children, we do not need to come as beggars. We are invited. God has no second-class children. He never holds us at a distance if we have met the conditions for approach.

It is important that we come with confidence. This is faith in action—faith that will not be denied. It is faith that takes God at His word and believes God to be as good as His word.

We demonstrate faith in God's faithfulness. We approach the throne—with confidence.

Mercy First

We are told to approach God's throne of grace to receive mercy and grace. I believe the order is significant.

Essentially, mercy relates to people who have done wrong—those who cannot claim their rights because they are unworthy or too weak to do so. There is an attitude in the world today that makes people strive to claim their rights. Someone says, "This is due to me" and "That is due to me." Or "Why didn't I get that?" and "I ought to have this." With that prevailing attitude, it is often hard for people to see that they need mercy. I thank God personally that from the time I came to know the Lord many years ago, I have never been in any doubt about one truth: I need God's mercy. I am clear about that no matter what situation I find myself in. I cannot just trust in my "rights"—they are not sufficient. I need God's mercy. It is so important for each of us to see that.

I am reminded of a friend of mine who is in full-time Christian ministry. Early in his life, he was a traveling sales-man—one who by his own admission was a rather reckless driver. He had received several tickets for exceeding the speed limit. This continued until one day he received a summons to the sheriff's office.

On his way to that appointment, he had a terrible feeling that he was going to have his license suspended. Of course, that would have been a very serious situation for him because it would take away his means of carrying on with his profession. On his way, he prepared what he was going to say when he was summoned before the sheriff. Here is what he said: "Sir, I'm not asking for justice. I'm asking for mercy."

To that, the sheriff replied, "No one has ever said that to me before!" The magistrate was so taken aback that, although my friend received a severe warning, he was permitted to retain his license.

That story has always stuck with me. I think that when we come to God, it would be much better if we came with that attitude: "I'm not asking for justice; I'm asking for mercy." I believe that when we come with that attitude, God will never withhold His mercy. One of the main reasons why people do not receive mercy is because they do not see their need of it.

Grace Next

The second benefit we come to the Lord for is grace. What is grace? Grace is what God will freely do for us beyond what we deserve. One essential characteristic of grace is that it cannot be deserved. Also, the grace of God is supernatural. It goes beyond all the limits of our natural ability.

Hebrews 4:16 says that we are to come "in time of need." That is so important. Are you in a situation of need? Is your situation desperate? Please do not let the devil fool you into thinking that your circumstances are too desperate. Do not allow him to tell you that it is too late to come, and there is nothing you can do about it. Why? Because God specifically invites you to come in time of need.

So, if your situation is desperate, let me recommend that you come to God's throne with confidence to receive these two benefits.

First of all, come for mercy. Never ask for your rights, because if you got what you rightfully deserve, you would be shocked. What you really deserve, you do not want. So come first for mercy.

Second, come for grace. Do not limit God regarding what He can do on your behalf. And remember—do not be dissuaded by the fact that your situation is desperate. That is just the right time to come.

Finally, remember that you are coming to a throne. On that throne is a King. In addition, the King you are approaching is the King of the universe. All authority and power—in heaven and on earth—is in His hands. He can answer any need we have. So let's take step number four. Let us draw near to the throne of grace.

7

Let Us Press On
to Maturity

THE FOUR KEYS we have learned all help us to attain a good
year and a good life, but we must not stop there. In fact, we
are not given that option. Here are the first four keys:

1. Let us fear
2. Let us be diligent
3. Let us hold fast our confession
4. Let us draw near to the throne of grace

Now, look at the fifth key, a point found in Hebrews 6.

KEY #5

"Let us press on to maturity"

Therefore leaving the elementary teaching about the Christ, let us press on to maturity.

Hebrews 6:1

Please note right from the beginning—it is tremendously important to see this truth—we *have* to do this. We are not given any other choice. Many believers have the impression that in the Christian life you can arrive. That you can settle down and say, "Now I'm there." But that is never true. To remain static in the spiritual life is the wrong choice. God expects us to move forward.

The Way

To understand the truth of the progressive nature of our relationship with Jesus Christ, let's look first at a single, penetrating verse from Proverbs 4:18: "The path of the righteous is like the light of dawn, that shines brighter and brighter until the full day."

The phrase *the path of the righteous* is absolutely general. It is not speaking about some particular believer or even some group of believers. Actually, it is speaking about every righteous person.

Please notice also that righteousness is a path. A path is something that we move along. A path is never designed for us to stand still in it, much less to sit down in it. Because righteousness is a path, it implies motion, progress and development.

Next, this passage says that this path is like the light of dawn. Dawn could be compared to the time when we first come to know the Lord in His glorious fullness as Savior and Lord. It is like a sunrise after the darkness. Coming to know Jesus is like a dawn that comes into our hearts.

But the dawn is not the end of God's purposes; it is the beginning. This verse says that the path is like the light of dawn that shines brighter and brighter until the full day. As we are walking in the path of righteousness, the light should always be getting brighter on our day. Each step—each day—the light should be brighter than it was before.

This verse in Proverbs 4 concludes with this phrase: *until the full day*. That is our destination—the height of noonday. God is not content that we would stop at less than the full brightness of the noonday sun. The dawn is our beginning point. The path is the way of progress. The light gets brighter and brighter. But no stopping place on the path is permitted until we reach the full day.

Advancing toward Maturity

Do you remember the biggest mistake that the Hebrews made? Like their forefathers they had become lazy and failed to listen for God's voice. That is why this particular *Let us* is so appropriate. The Hebrews were trusting their special privileges and resting in them; they had become lazy. They were just taking their status for granted. Look again at what the writer says to them:

> We have much to say about this, but it is hard to explain because you are slow to learn. In fact, though by this time you ought to be teachers, you need someone to teach you the elementary truths of God's word all over again. You need milk, not solid food! Anyone who lives on milk, being still an infant, is not acquainted with the teaching about righteousness. But solid food is for the mature, who by constant use have trained themselves to distinguish good from evil.
>
> Hebrews 5:11–14 NIV1984

The writer is saying here—and he is saying it pretty bluntly—"You're just spiritual infants. But you have no right to be infants at this stage in your Christian progress. You have had so many opportunities and so many years—you should have advanced to maturity by now."

In this same passage, the writer also explains the only way to advance to maturity. He says, "Solid food is for the mature, who by constant use have trained themselves to distinguish good from evil." According to that example, advancing to maturity along that path of righteousness, in which the light grows brighter day by day, comes in actual practice by constant use. It comes by training ourselves. It is not something we can take for granted or something that just happens automatically. It requires our application. That is why the second key is, "Let us be diligent." By constant use, we must train ourselves to distinguish good from evil if we are going to move forward in God.

It grieves me when I see large groups of Christians who seem to be absolutely unable to distinguish between what is truly spiritual, truly scriptural, and that which is just a fleshly presentation. They do not see that something with simply soulish appeal has no real lasting effect—and often no real basis in Scripture.

Unfortunately, multitudes of Christians are apparently taken in regularly by that kind of soulishness. They have not yet learned to distinguish good from evil. The remedy is to train ourselves by constant use and by practice. The only unfortunate alternative to such practice is arrested spiritual development—remaining in the condition of infants when we should be mature.

Five Ministries

God has made a special provision for attaining to spiritual maturity, and we need to know about it. It is stated in Paul's letter to the Ephesians:

It was he [the risen, ascended Christ] who gave some to be apostles, some to be prophets, some to be evangelists, and some to be pastors and teachers, to prepare God's people for works of service, so that the body of Christ may be built up until we all reach unity in the faith and in the knowledge of the Son of God and become mature, attaining to the whole measure of the fullness of Christ.

Ephesians 4:11–13 NIV1984

Five main ministries are mentioned here: apostles, prophets, evangelists, pastors and teachers. Starting with verse 12, we see the purpose of these ministries: "To prepare God's people for works of service, so that the body of Christ may be built up."

Please notice those two purposes. First, that God's people may be prepared for works of service. God's people cannot automatically do the work they are expected to do. They have to be prepared; they have to be trained. These five ministries have been given to do that training. The second purpose of these ministries is "so that the body of Christ may be built up."

Our vision expands as we go on in verse 13. We read: "until we all reach unity in the faith and in the knowledge of the Son of God and become mature." Do you see this truth? These ministries are placed within the Body of Christ to bring us into the unity of the faith and to bring us to maturity.

Paul concludes verse 13 with this thought: "attaining to the whole measure of the fullness of Christ." In order to attain this maturity, Jesus Christ, as head of the Church, has provided these five main ministries. Frankly, I believe that God's people will never attain maturity without this provision.

In verse 16 of that chapter, Paul, speaking about Christ again, says: "From him the whole body, joined and held together by every supporting ligament, grows and builds itself up in love, as each part does its work" (Ephesians 4:16 NIV1984).

The ultimate portrait of the Body of Christ painted here by Paul is not an assortment of separated, isolated individuals, each one doing his own thing. Rather, the result is to be one body held together by ligaments—by strong bands that hold it together—building itself up and growing. For that growth to happen, it is essential that each part of the Body does its work.

Two Requirements

God's program for coming to maturity has two main requirements. First, we must come under the discipline of the God-given ministries that Paul has just listed: apostles, prophets, evangelists, pastors and teachers. Without that discipline, without that oversight and without that instruction, I cannot see how God's people can ever attain to maturity. Jesus never made a provision that was not important—so I believe this provision is essential.

The second condition is that we must be part of a growing body, not just isolated individuals. In this same Ephesians 4 passage, Paul states the only possible alternative to a growing body—one that is very sad. If we do not follow God's program for maturity, we will be "infants, tossed back and forth by the waves, and blown here and there by every wind of teaching and by the cunning and craftiness of men in their deceitful scheming" (Ephesians 4:14 NIV1984).

You see, if we do not come under these ministries—if we do not become part of a body and accept this scriptural discipline—Paul says the only alternative is that we will remain infants. We will be "tossed back and forth, blown here and there by every wind of teaching."

I know many believers like that. Every year they have a new fad, a new doctrine and often a new teacher to provide the fad—"by the cunning and craftiness of men in their deceitful scheming." Instead, they ought to come under the discipline of the legitimate ministries Jesus has given as gifts, and be part of a body. That is the only way to maturity.

Let me ask you a personal question. How about you? Are you under discipline? Are you part of a body of believers? Are you fulfilling the mandate of this fifth key? Are you advancing—pressing on—to maturity?

A *free* Derek Prince resource for you!

To further introduce you to the unique ministry of one of the great Bible teachers of our time, Derek Prince Ministries would like to send you one of his most acclaimed, timeless teachings.

Derek Prince's message on audio CD entitled "Do You Realize How Valuable You Are?" has helped countless people around the world discover the freedom, power and purpose that flow from a revelation of your worth to your heavenly Father.

Simply fill out and return this card, and we'll get it right out to you!

☐ **Yes,** please send me the Derek Prince teaching
"Do You Realize How Valuable You Are?" on audio CD. CD411

name:

address:

city: state: zip:

e-mail:

www.derekprince.org

[f] [t] @DPMUSA

8

Let Us Draw Near
to the Most Holy Place

OUR SIXTH KEY for successful living is found in Hebrews 10. It is interesting to me that in almost every one of these keys, the text begins with the word *therefore*. In other words, we see a logical unfolding, a sequence of thought. Here are our first five keys:

1. Let us fear
2. Let us be diligent
3. Let us hold fast our confession

4. Let us draw near to the throne of grace
5. Let us press on to maturity

Have you placed these first five squarely in your memory? If so, let's move on now and look at the sixth key.

KEY #6

"Let us draw near to the Most Holy Place"

Therefore, brothers, since we have confidence to enter the Most Holy Place by the blood of Jesus, by a new and living way opened for us through the curtain, that is, his body, and since we have a great priest over the house of God, let us draw near to God with a sincere heart in full assurance of faith, having our hearts sprinkled to cleanse us from a guilty conscience and having our bodies washed with pure water.

Hebrews 10:19–22 NIV1984

The content of this verse sounds similar to the fourth key, but there is an important distinction. That one was: "Let us draw near to the throne of grace." This sixth key is: "Let us draw near to God." The distinction is made clear in the context of Hebrews 10:19 and the follow-up in verse 22: "Since we have confidence to enter the Most Holy Place . . . let us draw near to God." This suggests that drawing near to God is equivalent to entering the Most Holy Place.

In light of that truth, look again at these two statements. "Let us draw near to the throne" (Key #4) means that we can come for the help we need—for mercy and for grace. But "Let us draw near to the Most Holy Place" (Key #6) means that we draw near to God Himself. I believe that this key opens the way to go much further. Not merely do we come to the throne for help, but we come because we are invited to take our place with Christ on the throne. It is by taking our place with Him that we enter into the Most Holy Place.

The Tabernacle Pattern

The author of Hebrews uses descriptive language here based on the pattern of the Tabernacle of Moses. Put simply, three main areas comprised the Tabernacle. First was the Outer Court, an open courtyard bordered by curtains. Any Israelite could enter this area. Then, within this courtyard on the western end, was the Tabernacle itself—a portable tent held up by a wooden framework. Inside the first curtain of the tent was the Holy Place. Only priests could enter this chamber. At the farther end, beyond the second curtain, was the Most Holy Place. This chamber could be entered only by the high priest once a year—on the Day of Atonement.

Our destination is the Most Holy Place, beyond the second curtain.

The only furniture in the Most Holy Place, as it was designed by God, was the Ark of the Covenant. This was a box made out of acacia wood that was completely covered with gold. The Ark was topped with what was called the Mercy Seat, or the place of propitiation. Inside the Ark were the two tablets containing the Ten Commandments, but these were covered by the Mercy Seat. This placement indicates that through Christ's propitiation on our behalf, the Law has been covered by mercy.

On the ends of the Mercy Seat were two cherubs facing one another. They were looking toward the center of the Mercy Seat with their wings stretched out over them and their wing tips touching in the center.

The Mercy Seat is God's throne. It is important for us to remember that God sits on a throne of mercy. His mercy covers the Law. The two cherubs with their faces turned inward toward one another, their wing tips touching, represent the place of fellowship. So, the Mercy Seat is a place of mercy, a place of fellowship—but it is also a throne, the seat of God as King.

There was no representation of God Himself in that piece of furniture—which, of course, was forbidden by Law for the Israelites. But God did come into the Most Holy Place and take His seat. He came in the form of the *Shekinah* glory—the visible, palpable presence of Almighty God. Without that glory, the Most Holy Place was in total darkness. There was no natural or artificial illumination. When the *Shekinah*, the glorious presence of God, came in, it was the sign that God was taking His place on the throne.

The sixth *Let us* statement, then, invites us into the Most Holy Place. We are welcomed to draw near to God. We are, in fact, invited to take our place with Christ on the throne. This passage in Hebrews 10 also tells us that we are to come by "a new and living way." What is the new and living way? It is Jesus. We see a direct comparison of Jesus' life and ministry—the "new and living way"—to the Most Holy Place.

Four Requirements

Even though we are invited to enter the Most Holy Place, the writer of Hebrews says that we must fulfill certain requirements in order to approach the Mercy Seat and the throne.

1. A Sincere Heart

We approach God with our hearts, not with our heads. God is not the answer to an intellectual riddle, but He does meet a longing heart. It must be a sincere heart, without any pretensions or hypocrisy. We have to expose ourselves to God just as we are and not try to cover up anything or pretend to be different than we are. We must be open and honest with Him.

2. A Full Assurance of Faith

In the next chapter of Hebrews, we read: "Without faith it is impossible to please [God], for he who comes to God must believe" (Hebrews 11:6 NKJV).

We see from this passage that we must come with faith in God's faithfulness; in other words, we come not in our own ability or righteousness, but with absolute faith in God's faithfulness.

3. Our Hearts Sprinkled from an Evil Conscience

An "evil conscience" comes from wrong and sinful deeds we have committed in the past. Through the blood of Jesus, however, we can receive assurance that all those evil deeds in the past have been forgiven and that our hearts are pure from sin. We can have our hearts sprinkled from an evil conscience through the blood of Jesus.

4. Our Bodies Washed with Pure Water

In his first epistle, John tells us that Jesus came by water and by blood (see 1 John 5:6). In these two conditions, we see the blood that sprinkles from an evil conscience and the water that washes our bodies. I believe *water* refers to Christian baptism. In every place where it is explained in the New Testament, Christian baptism is depicted as sharing in the death, burial and resurrection of Jesus Christ.

This confirms for us that "the new and living way" is Jesus. It is the act of coming and partaking of His death, His burial and His resurrection. As we approach the Mercy Seat, we identify with everything that Jesus went through in dying for our sins.

Identification with Jesus

What, then, does it mean to be seated with Jesus? It means to be enthroned—to share the throne with Him.

But because of his great love for us, God, who is rich in mercy, made us alive with Christ even when we were dead in transgressions—it is by grace you have been saved. And God raised us up with Christ and seated us with him in the heavenly realms in Christ Jesus.

Ephesians 2:4–6 NIV1984

Notice the three stages of identification with Jesus. First, we are "made alive." Second, we are "raised up" or resurrected. And third, we are "seated with Him." Where is Jesus seated? On the throne.

Once we see our identification with Jesus, we are invited to follow Him all the way. Since He is the "new and living way," we can be made alive with Him, and we can be resurrected with Him. But we do not need to stop there. We can also be enthroned with Him.

In the pattern of the Tabernacle, the first curtain represents what we enter into through sharing in the resurrection of Jesus. The second curtain that leads to the Most Holy Place represents what we enter into through sharing in the ascension of Jesus.

Jesus was not merely resurrected; subsequently, He was raised up to heaven to the throne. That is where God wants us. God does not want us to stop short in this new and living way until we have reached the throne—until we are sharing the throne with Jesus, seated with Him in heavenly places. That is our destination.

9

Let Us Hold Fast Our Confession without Wavering

DOES IT EVER FEEL as though you have lost sight of God? Does evil seem to be winning in your life? If the answer is yes, take special note of this all-important seventh key.

First, though, let's review our first six keys:

1. Let us fear
2. Let us be diligent
3. Let us hold fast our confession
4. Let us draw near to the throne of grace

5. Let us press on to maturity
6. Let us draw near to the Most Holy Place

The seventh key is found, like the previous one, in Hebrews 10.

KEY #7

"Let us hold fast our confession without wavering"

Let us hold fast the confession of our hope without wavering, for He who promised is faithful.

Hebrews 10:23

Let's take a moment to review what we have learned about confession. First, *confession* means "saying the same as God." Confessing our faith, then, is saying the same with our mouths that God says in His Word. It is making our words agree with the written Word of God in every point. Generally, as we advance in the spiritual life, our confession comes closer to being in complete agreement with the Word of God in every area of our lives.

Second, it is through our confession that we are linked to Jesus as our High Priest. One of the main themes of Hebrews is that Jesus is our High Priest in heaven. He is there on our behalf in the presence of God the Father—to represent us, to present our petitions, to intercede on our behalf and to make good every right confession that we make.

This is brought out in Hebrews 3:1: "Therefore, holy brethren, partakers of a heavenly calling, consider Jesus, the Apostle and High Priest of our confession."

In other words, our confession enlists the ministry of Jesus as High Priest on our behalf. If we make the right confession, Jesus is obligated in His eternal faithfulness to see that the confession is made good. If we fail to make the right confession or if we make no confession at all, we silence the lips of our High Priest. We give Him no opportunity to minister as High Priest on our behalf. We can see, therefore, that there is tremendous importance in confession.

The Sequence of Confessing

There is much to learn from the way this theme of confession is built up in the epistle to the Hebrews.

First, in Hebrews 3:1, we are admonished to make the right confession: Jesus is the Apostle and High Priest of our confession. We then remember the related key we studied in Hebrews 4:14—the third key: "Since then we have a great high priest who has passed through the heavens, Jesus the Son of God, let us hold fast our confession." In speaking of Jesus as our High Priest, Scripture immediately goes on to emphasize our confession—in other words, our confession enlists His ministry on our behalf as our High Priest. And in Hebrews

4:14, we are admonished to "hold fast" our confession. We must not change what we have said. We need to keep making the words of our mouths agree with the Word of God.

Thus, we come to the next step in this sequence, the seventh key: "Let us hold fast the confession of our hope without wavering" (Hebrews 10:23). Notice the two added words: *without wavering*.

If we look through these passages of Hebrews in correct order, we see that, in respect to our confession, there are three successive stages. First, we make the confession. Second, having made it, we hold fast; we do not change. Third, we hold it fast without wavering.

Why do you think *without wavering* is put in? What does it imply? To me, these words imply—not merely on the basis of logic but on the basis of personal experience—that when we make the right confession, we are going to encounter negative forces and pressures that will come against us. Even though we have made the right confession and are holding it fast, there may come a time when the pressure increases. At that time, it may seem that all the forces of Satan and all the powers of darkness are turned loose against us, tempting us to let go of our confession.

The Right Response

This is the very point at which the writer of Hebrews tells us, "Don't let go. Hold fast—without wavering." The darker the situation, the greater the problem and the stronger the pressures, the more important it is for us to hold fast without wavering. Why? Because "He who promised is faithful" (Hebrews 10:23).

You may feel that God is behind the clouds, out of sight, and you have no idea what He is doing. But Scripture says He is faithful. Whether you see Him or not, whether you understand or not, He is faithful. He is committed to His Word, and He is our High Priest. If we hold fast our confession *without wavering*, He will do His job as our High Priest.

Compare what we have just observed with this simple statement in 2 Corinthians 5:7: "For we walk by faith, not by sight." Clearly, you can see that there is opposition between faith and sight. The natural man walks by sight—he trusts his senses, and he believes only what his senses tell him. But in our spiritual lives as Christians, we should not trust our senses. We walk by faith.

Faith relates us to an unseen, eternal realm where reality does not change. The world of the senses is always changing—it is temporary, unstable and unreliable. But through faith we relate to a different world—a world of eternal realities and eternal truths. As we relate to that world by faith, we hold fast our confession without wavering.

The pressures God permits to come into our lives determine whether we are trusting our senses or our faith. If we change our confession because of the darkness, then we are going by our senses and not by faith.

For faith, there is no darkness. Faith sees with an inner spiritual eye into a realm that does not change. Faith gazes upon a High Priest who is reliable and constant.

The Example of Abraham

In connection with this principle of making and holding the right confession without wavering, look for a moment at the example of Abraham as he is portrayed in Romans 4. I think that Abraham is one of the best examples of holding fast without wavering. This is what Paul says about Abraham:

> Without weakening in his faith, he faced the fact that his body was as good as dead—since he was about a hundred years old—and that Sarah's womb was also dead. Yet he did not waver through unbelief regarding the promise of God, but was strengthened in his faith and gave glory to God, being fully persuaded that God had power to do what he had promised. This is why "it was credited to him as righteousness."
>
> Romans 4:19–22 NIV1984

We see from this example that real faith faces facts. Any attitude that is not willing to look at the real facts is not real faith. Abraham did not try to deceive himself or picture the situation differently from what it was. With his senses he saw that his body and Sarah's womb were as good as dead. But then he decided not to trust only in his senses.

Abraham is called "the father of all who believe" (Romans 4:11), and we are exhorted to follow in his steps of faith. We are required to walk that same path of faith. How? We lay hold of the promise of God, we make our confession, and then we hold our confession fast without wavering.

We are not to be deterred by what our senses reveal, but to look beyond the senses and the seen things into the unseen realm—to see by faith our faithful High Priest, there at God's right hand.

Don't Be Double-Minded

In this connection, listen to what James says in his epistle. Many Christians fail at this point. They make a confession; they hold it fast; but when the pressures build up, they do not hold it fast without wavering.

> But when [a believer] asks, he must believe and not doubt, because he who doubts is like a wave of the sea, blown and tossed by the wind. That man should not think he will receive anything from the Lord; he is a double-minded man, unstable in all he does.
>
> James 1:6–8 NIV1984

This is the person who wavers: a person who starts to ask, starts to pray or starts to believe—but who does not hold fast without wavering. That person is tossed to and fro, blown about by the winds and the waves. Scripture says about such a person—and this is a very solemn warning—"that man should not think he will receive anything from the Lord."

By wavering, we can forfeit our blessings and lose the benefit of Christ's ministry on our behalf as our High Priest. What is the remedy? "Let us hold fast our confession without wavering."

10

Let Us Consider One Another

ARE YOU SEEING the logical progression to the good decisions we are making? These benefit us individually, but, as we have seen, they also apply to our relationships with other believers, helping us hold fast our confession as we mature in the faith. We will learn more about the relational aspect of the keys in this chapter.

First, here are the seven keys we have studied thus far:

1. Let us fear
2. Let us be diligent
3. Let us hold fast our confession

4. Let us draw near to the throne of grace
5. Let us press on to maturity
6. Let us draw near to the Most Holy Place
7. Let us hold fast our confession without wavering

In this chapter, we move on to the eighth key. Like the two previous ones, it is also found in Hebrews 10. In order to get an understanding of the context, let's look at these three verses.

KEY #8

"Let us consider one another"

And let us consider how to stimulate one another to love and good deeds, not forsaking our own assembling together, as is the habit of some, but encouraging one another; and all the more, as you see the day drawing near. For if we go on sinning willfully after receiving the knowledge of the truth, there no longer remains a sacrifice for sins.

Hebrews 10:24–26

The translation used above for these verses is a good one. In the original Greek, however, the order is reversed. In Greek, this reads: "Let us consider one another, how to stimulate to love and good deeds." That brings out the true essence of this particular key. It is: "Let us consider one another." We are to consider one another from the point of view of how we can bring out the best in each other.

So many people today are shut up in the prison of self. Their basic problem is self-centeredness. I have never met a self-centered person who was truly happy, nor who enjoyed true peace. In fact, the more you concentrate on yourself, the more you worry about yourself, the more you seek to please yourself, the more your problems will increase.

You must first be released from that prison of self-centeredness. Would you like to know one scriptural way to be released? Here it is: Stop worrying about yourself. Stop caring for yourself all the time. Stop fighting for yourself. Instead, start to consider your fellow believers. "Let us consider one another."

The Example of Jesus

In Philippians, Paul sets the example of Jesus before us as one we need to follow. Jesus' example is applicable to this key, as we can see from all that Paul says in Philippians 2. He starts with this instruction:

> Do nothing from selfishness or empty conceit, but with humility of mind let each of you regard one another as more important than himself; do not merely look out for your own personal interests, but also for the interests of others.
>
> Philippians 2:3–4

What Paul recommends here is the exact opposite of looking out for your own personal interests. The release comes to you as you look out for the interests of others—as you become more concerned about others than yourself.

Then Paul talks about the need to follow the example of Jesus. He goes on to say:

Have this attitude in yourselves which was also in Christ Jesus, who, although He existed in the form of God, did not regard equality with God a thing to be grasped, but emptied Himself, taking the form of a bondservant.

Philippians 2:5–7

At the beginning of this book, we talked about the vital role of attitude in the overall process. We said that our attitude determines our approach and our approach determines the outcome. Here, then, is an attitude that we need to cultivate: "Have this attitude in yourself which was also in Christ Jesus."

What was His attitude? The Greek literally describes the attitude of Jesus as one of "a slave." Jesus, who was Lord of all, emptied Himself of everything and was willing to become a servant—a bondservant, a slave. That is the attitude Paul says we need to imitate.

We find a very beautiful parallel passage in Galatians 5:13–14:

For you were called to freedom, brethren; only do not turn your freedom into an opportunity for the flesh [that is, to gratify your own fleshly and selfish desires], but through

80

love serve one another. For the whole Law is fulfilled in one word, in the statement, "You shall love your neighbor as yourself."

The way for us *not* to indulge our fleshly nature, *not* to yield to selfishness and *not* to become shut up in that prison of self is to look outward to others. "Through love serve one another" is exactly what the Holy Spirit is emphasizing to God's people today.

Many people talk about serving the Lord, but they never serve their fellow believers. Can you really serve the Lord if you are not willing to serve your fellow believers? The Lord comes to us in the members of His Body—so our attitude toward those members is really our attitude toward the Lord Himself.

The Example of Paul

In this connection of being willing to serve others, let's look at a statement Paul wrote to the Corinthian Christians. Bear in mind, Paul was by background a strict, observant, orthodox Jew. He had the qualifications to be a rabbi. He was a Pharisee. His approach to righteousness was that it caused him to separate himself from other people, regarding others as on a lower level. Please bear in mind also that the Corinthians were regarded basically as the dregs of the earth. In his letters to them, Paul says that some of them had been homosexuals, some prostitutes, some drunkards and some revilers (see 1 Corinthians 6:9–11). Corinth was one of the major seaports of the ancient world and, as so often happens in seaport towns, immorality was widespread.

Imagine how this "Pharisee of Pharisees" would have looked down upon these people! When he came to know Jesus, however, the most wonderful change took place in his nature. In that context, consider this astonishing statement by Paul: "For we do not preach ourselves but Christ Jesus as Lord, and ourselves as your bond-servants for Jesus' sake" (2 Corinthians 4:5). Here is a proud Pharisee saying, "We are your slaves for the sake of Jesus." To the Corinthians—of all people!

Notice the three steps Paul outlines. First, dethrone self: "not ourselves." Second, enthrone Christ: "Christ Jesus the Lord." Third, serve others: "We are your bondservants for Jesus' sake." How do we escape from self-centeredness? The process Paul describes is the answer to that question.

Serving Is a Skill

What does it mean for us to serve? I must point out here that serving is a skill we have to acquire. It does not just happen, and it is not ours by nature. Take the example of a waiter. A waiter is one who, in a sense, is called to serve. But a waiter needs to be trained.

I have a friend who was a waiter, and he explained to me once what is involved in being a good waiter. In his description

I saw a marvelous example of the training we need to serve one another. Serving is a skill we have to acquire. We must study others to find out what produces a positive or negative response. We have to find out what will provoke them to love and good deeds, not to the opposite. This requires practice, training and discipline.

It also requires the right environment. You see, after saying, "Let us consider how to stimulate one another to love and good deeds," Paul goes on to say, "not forsaking our own assembling together, as is the habit of some, but encouraging one another; and all the more, as you see the day drawing near" (Hebrews 10:25). The right environment is expressed in the words *our own assembling together*. It means that close, committed, regular fellowship is the environment in which we can be trained to serve one another.

In the next verse, the writer of Hebrews states the disastrous alternative. Immediately after the warning against forsaking our own assembling together, he says this: "For if we go on sinning willfully after receiving the knowledge of the truth, there no longer remains a sacrifice for sins" (Hebrew 10:26).

It is no accident that these words follow. The implication is that if we do not stay in the right environment, if we are not in close, committed, regular fellowship, we will go back to sinning. The only safe way to learn to be servants as Paul taught and Jesus exemplified is to stay in fellowship, learn to serve and learn to consider other people. That is the essence of our eighth key: "Let us consider one another."

11

Let Us Run with Endurance the Race

How is your memorization process going? Here are the eight successive keys that we have addressed thus far:

1. Let us fear
2. Let us be diligent
3. Let us hold fast our confession
4. Let us draw near to the throne of grace
5. Let us press on to maturity
6. Let us draw near to the Most Holy Place

7. Let us hold fast our confession without wavering
8. Let us consider one another

We now come to the ninth key, which is found in the opening verses of Hebrews 12. We will begin by looking at the first two verses of that chapter.

KEY #9

"Let us run with endurance the race"

Therefore, since we have so great a cloud of witnesses surrounding us, let us also lay aside every encumbrance, and the sin which so easily entangles us, and let us run with endurance the race that is set before us, fixing our eyes on Jesus, the author and perfecter of faith, who for the joy set before Him endured the cross, despising the shame, and has sat down at the right hand of the throne of God.

Hebrews 12:1–2

This ninth key is found in verse 1: "Let us run with endurance the race that is set before us." Because of the circumstances of the English translation, I need to add a word of explanation about that verse. In the English translation, there are actually two *Let us* phrases in that one verse, which is a perfectly legitimate translation. In the original Greek, however, the first phrase *lay aside every encumbrance* is not in a form that includes *Let us*. Instead it reads like this: "Laying aside every encumbrance, let us run with endurance the race." The real *Let us* phrase upon which we need to focus is: "Let us run with endurance the race that is set before us."

Here and elsewhere in the New Testament, the Christian life is compared to a race. This analogy implies that there is a specific course marked out for us in advance, and success in the Christian life consists in completing the course in accordance with the rules of the competition. Since a race is set before us, I want to point out four conditions for success. Each one of these is found in the New Testament.

A Right Mental Attitude

The first condition for success in life's race is exemplified by the words of Paul in Philippians 3:10–11 where, speaking about his relationship to Jesus Christ, he says: "That I may know Him, and the power of His resurrection and the fellowship of His sufferings, being conformed to His death; in order that I may attain to the resurrection from the dead."

You see, Paul has a specific objective. Elsewhere he says that he does not run aimlessly (see 1 Corinthians 9:26–27). He has an aim before him. He knows what the goal is—and this determines his mental attitude. Then he goes on to say in Philippians 3:12: "Not that I have already obtained it, or have already become perfect [or complete], but I press on in order that I may lay hold of that for which also I was laid hold of by Christ Jesus."

Paul has this clear vision: Christ laid hold of him for a purpose, and the fulfilling of that purpose means he must relate to the purpose. He has to be determined that Christ's purpose for him will become his purpose. He continues:

> Brethren, I do not regard myself as having laid hold of it yet; but one thing I do: forgetting what lies behind and reaching forward to what lies ahead, I press on toward the goal for the prize of the upward call of God in Christ Jesus.
>
> Philippians 3:13–14

Please notice: The phrase *I press on* occurs twice in these passages. I believe that is the mental attitude you and I need to share: "I press on. I have a goal. I haven't arrived, but I know where I'm headed." The last time Paul uses the phrase, he says, "I press on toward the goal for the prize of the upward call of God in Christ Jesus." There is a reward for those who successfully complete the race. It is important for us always to keep the goal in mind, reminding ourselves that we do not want to lose our God-appointed reward.

Self-Control

The second condition for success in this race is self-control. Again, this is illustrated by the words of Paul in 1 Corinthians. Here he compares the Christian life to competing in an athletic contest. This is a really good parallel—one that is vivid for us today, because many of us follow sports. The same principle still applies.

> Do you not know that those who run in a race all run, but only one receives the prize? Run in such a way that you may win. And everyone who competes in the games exercises self-control in all things. They then do it to receive a perishable wreath [that is, the prize], but we an imperishable [wreath].
>
> 1 Corinthians 9:24–25

The objective in racing is to win the prize. If we are going to win the race, we must meet the condition of self-control. It is obvious that athletes who wish to participate in world competitions today have to exercise the most rigorous self-control. They have to "go into training"—controlling what they eat, how much they sleep, the amount and type of exercise that they undergo. Controlling one's psychology is also important, building up the right kind of attitude. Negative thoughts must be put aside to maintain a positive attitude in order to achieve victory.

All this is equally true for us as Christians in our race. We cannot win the race without self-control.

Endurance

The third condition for victory in this race is stated in the verse from Hebrews 12:1, which we have already cited.

What is that condition? Endurance. This is one quality that is essential in Christian character if we are going to achieve real spiritual success and fulfillment. Endurance must be cultivated.

The opposite of endurance is giving up or quitting. Christians cannot afford to be quitters. When God commits something to us, we must set our faces and go through with it.

There is a close relationship between self-control and endurance; that is why I put them in that order. In actual fact, without self-control we will not achieve endurance. We have to master our weaknesses. Otherwise, every time we are tested in the area of endurance, some weakness—emotional, psychological or physical—will get us down. What will be the result? We will give up just at the point where we should have been holding on and enduring.

Eyes Fixed on Jesus

The fourth condition for success is to have our eyes fixed on Jesus. This is stated in Hebrews 12:2: "Fixing our eyes on Jesus, the author and perfecter of [our] faith, who for the joy set before Him endured the cross."

In other words, we cannot run the race in our own self-reliance. *Looking to Jesus* means that He is our example. We put our confidence in Him. Jesus is the author, the beginning of our faith. He is also the perfecter, the one who will bring us through to victory.

Testimony of a Victor

The apostle Paul was a victor. Here is his testimony in 2 Timothy 4:7–8:

> I have fought the good fight, I have finished the course, I have kept the faith; in the future there is laid up for me the crown of righteousness, which the Lord, the righteous Judge, will award to me on that day; and not only to me, but also to all who have loved His appearing.

Paul knows he has won the race, he has finished the course, and he knows the prize is there waiting for him. That is a glorious testimony, and it can be your testimony and my testimony if we will meet the conditions.

There are men and women in the world today—I have known a number of them—of whom the same testimony is true. They completed their course. They can say, like Paul, "I've fought the good fight. I've finished the course. I've kept the faith." May we be able to say the same! That will be possible if we take hold of the ninth key: "Let us run with endurance the race."

12

Let Us Show Gratitude

THERE IS A RIGHT WAY to approach God, and a wrong way. This is something else about which we have no option. We have to come before this holy God with the right attitude. The understanding of that right attitude is the subject of this chapter.

How is your memorization of the keys coming?

1. Let us fear
2. Let us be diligent
3. Let us hold fast our confession

4. Let us draw near to the throne of grace
5. Let us press on to maturity
6. Let us draw near to the Most Holy Place
7. Let us hold fast our confession without wavering
8. Let us consider one another
9. Let us run with endurance the race

Like the ninth key, the tenth key is also found in Hebrews 12. It comes near the end of that chapter.

KEY #10

"Let us show gratitude"

Therefore, since we receive a kingdom which cannot be shaken, let us show gratitude, by which we may offer to God an acceptable service with reverence and awe; for our God is a consuming fire.

Hebrews 12:28–29

The King James Version translates *Let us show gratitude* as *Let us have grace*. We see in this the connection between *grace* and *thanks*. The King James translation is a literal translation of the words; likewise, the phrase *to have grace* is commonly used in Greek to express the giving of thanks. This concept brings out the connection between grace and thanks—one that is found in various modern languages. The French, for instance, say, *Grâce á Dieu,* "Thanks to God." In both Italian and Spanish, the word for *thank you* is taken from the word *grace.* In Italian it is *grazie* and in Spanish it is *gracias.*

So you see, in these and other languages there is a connection between grace and thanks. May I tell you something that I believe strongly? You cannot have the grace of God in your life unless you practice giving thanks. Grace and thanks go together. There is nothing more ungracious than an unthankful person, whereas a thankful person will always experience the grace of God.

Two Requirements

We need to see that God requires two responses from us as His people. First, He requires that we appreciate what He does for us. Second, He requires that we *express* our appreciation—and that is crucial for us to understand.

There are some people who really are grateful to God, but they never take time to tell God how grateful they are. Please let me ask you a question. How would you feel as a parent if your children never thanked you in spite of all that you did for them? You probably would not like it at all. What if they never said thank you or showed their gratitude, but just accepted everything you did for them as if it were theirs by right? How would you feel if they just took all you did for granted? Unfortunately, many of God's children treat God like that, and it is not pleasing in His sight. We are required to appreciate what God does for us. Additionally, we are required to express our appreciation.

One of my favorite Scriptures is Proverbs 3:6: "In all your ways acknowledge Him [God], and He shall direct your paths" (NKJV). I have learned by experience that if I pause at every stage in life to acknowledge God, I can be confident that He will continue to direct my path.

You may ask: "How can I acknowledge God?" The simplest and the best way is simply by thanking Him—thanking Him for all He has done; thanking Him for His faithfulness. When you acknowledge Him in this way, you will get the assurance immediately that He is going to go on being faithful. Just as He has helped and guided in the past, He will guide in the future. But the key to this assurance is acknowledging Him by our thanksgiving.

God's Unshaken Kingdom

The writer of Hebrews gives us the background of this exhortation to thankfulness. Looking at the previous three verses of Hebrews 12, we read this rather solemn warning:

See to it that you do not refuse Him who is speaking [to us. And then a parallel is taken from the Old Testament, when God spoke to the people of Israel through Moses:] For if those did not escape when they refused him who warned them on earth, much less shall we [believers in the New Testament] escape who turn away from Him who warns from heaven. And His voice shook the earth then, but now He has promised, saying, "Yet once more I will shake not only the earth, but also the heaven." And this expression, "Yet once more," denotes the removing of those things which can be shaken, as of created things, in order that those things which cannot be shaken may remain.

Hebrews 12:25–27

This is the background of the exhortation to show gratitude. We are in a world that is crumbling—it is falling apart. All around us we see distress, uncertainty, perplexity, confusion, hatred, division, war, fear—not merely in one nation, but in all nations of the earth. To a greater or lesser degree, these conditions continue and, indeed, grow worse. God says, "There's coming a time when I'm going to shake once more not only the earth but also the heavens." This "once more" indicates this is going to be the final shaking. In this final shaking, everything that can be shaken will be removed. But in light of this, the writer of Hebrews says: "Since we receive a kingdom which cannot be shaken, let us show gratitude" (Hebrews 12:28).

That, my friend, is the appropriate response to the particular privileges and benefits we have in God. We are not dependent on a shakable kingdom. We have an eternal Kingdom, an unshakable Kingdom, the Kingdom of God Himself. That Kingdom is "righteousness and peace and joy in the Holy Spirit" (Romans 14:17).

In the midst of all that is going on around us—all the shaking, all the threatening, all the alarms, all the fears and all the inadequate and insufficient remedies that only temporarily stop the gap—in the midst of all this, we have an unshakable Kingdom. We have peace, security, purpose. There is only one appropriate response to that realization: It is thankfulness. "Therefore, since we receive a kingdom which cannot be shaken, let us show gratitude." Let us express our thanks to God!

An Acceptable Service

Not only is thankfulness or gratitude the appropriate response to what God has done and is doing for us—not only is it something we owe God and need to pay—but thankfulness or gratitude or the expression of our appreciation does something in our spirits that nothing else can do. Here is how I express it: Thankfulness releases our spirits for acceptable worship and service. That is why the writer of Hebrews says, "Let us show gratitude, that we may offer to God an acceptable service, with reverence and awe."

Without gratitude, our service to God will not be acceptable. It is that "attitude of gratitude" that makes our service acceptable and releases our spirits. An unthankful person is bound up in himself. He is self-centered. He really cannot know true liberation. But thankfulness releases our spirits.

Look at what Paul says in 1 Thessalonians 5:18–19: "In everything give thanks; for this is God's will for you in Christ Jesus. Do not quench the Spirit." That is a clear commandment. If we fail to give thanks, we are being disobedient. If we do not give thanks, we are out of the will of God.

Failing to give thanks quenches the Spirit. The only release for the Spirit, to serve God acceptably, is through thanksgiving.

A Consuming Fire

As part of this teaching on showing gratitude, we want to take special note of the closing warning in Hebrews 12:29: "For our God is a consuming fire." Here is what the writer is saying: "We have to approach this holy, awe-inspiring God with the right attitude—with a humble, thankful heart."

As we consider the world in these last days, we must acknowledge that a "shaking" is coming. With it is the disintegration of character, morality and standards. Paul says:

> But mark this: There will be terrible times in the last days. People will be lovers of themselves, lovers of money, boastful, proud, abusive, disobedient to their parents, ungrateful, unholy, without love, unforgiving, slanderous, without self-control, brutal, not lovers of the good, treacherous, rash, conceited, lovers of pleasure rather than lovers of God—having a form of godliness but denying its power. Have nothing to do with them.
>
> 2 Timothy 3:1–5 NIV1984

What a terrible list of moral defects and character degeneration that is going to mark the close of this age! If you go over that list, I think you will find that most of these character defects are conspicuous in our contemporary culture. Right in the middle of that list, it says, "disobedient to their parents, ungrateful, unholy, without love." Please notice that association. The ungrateful are right next door to the unholy. You cannot be holy and be ungrateful.

Since our God is a consuming fire, and He requires that we serve Him with holiness (which is appropriate), then we have to serve Him with gratitude. We must come to Him with thankfulness.

Look at those words once more: "Let us show gratitude, that we may serve Him acceptably, with reverence and godly fear."

13

Let Us Go Out to Him

NOT ONLY MUST we have the right attitude toward God, but also we must have the right attitude toward the world. This world is not our home. How, then, do we live in it successfully?

First, here are the ten keys that bring us to this point:

1. Let us fear
2. Let us be diligent
3. Let us hold fast our confession
4. Let us draw near to the throne of grace

5. Let us press on to maturity
6. Let us draw near to the Most Holy Place
7. Let us hold fast our confession without wavering
8. Let us consider one another
9. Let us run with endurance the race
10. Let us show gratitude

Our next key, number eleven out of twelve, is found in Hebrews 13.

KEY #11

"Let us go out to Him"

Therefore Jesus also, that He might sanctify the people through His own blood, suffered outside the gate. Hence, let us go out to Him outside the camp, bearing His reproach. For here we do not have a lasting city, but we are seeking the city which is to come.

Hebrews 13:12–14

This eleventh key deals with our attitude and our relationship to this present world. The core verse for this step is telling us that our home is not in this world. We do not have any enduring place here. The world rejected Jesus—it drove Him out of the city and crucified Him outside the gate.

Scripture always emphasizes the fact that the crucifixion took place outside the city wall. Jesus was absolutely rejected. He was put out of society. The world did not want Him. You and I both know that the way the world treated Jesus, sooner or later, in one way or another, is going to be the way the world will treat you and me as believers. We must be willing to go out to Him to the place of crucifixion—the place of rejection and shame, bearing His reproach.

The Reward of Reproach

Elsewhere in Hebrews, we read the testimony that the reproach of Christ is greater riches than all the treasures of Egypt (see Hebrews 11:26). His reproach becomes our glory. Then the writer gives a beautiful reason: "For here we do not have a lasting city, but we are seeking the city which is to come" (Hebrews 13:14). Other people might think this earthly existence is permanent; we know it is not.

I like this translation, which talks about "*the* city we are seeking." There is one specific, particular city that is the destination and the home of all true believers. That is where we really belong.

Two chapters earlier, in Hebrews 11, the writer provides a kind of honor roll of many of the great saints of the Old Testament, emphasizing their faith. He says about them:

All these died in faith, without receiving the promises, but having seen them and having welcomed them from a distance, and having confessed that they were strangers and exiles on the earth. For those who say such things make it clear that they are seeking a country of their own. And indeed if they had been thinking of that country from which they went out, they would have had opportunity to return. But as it is, they desire a better country, that is a heavenly one. Therefore God is not ashamed to be called their God; for He has prepared a city for them.

Hebrews 11:13–16

I am gripped by the words that are written there—that these forerunners in the faith, who are our examples in so many ways, confessed that they were strangers and exiles in this earth. They did not really belong; the earth was not their home. And then it says that they were seeking a country of their own. Those words have a poignant meaning for me.

It so happens that in my life I have had to deal with quite a number of people who were classified "stateless"—people who did not have a country, who did not own a passport. I thank God that by His grace I was able to help a number of them. I also know something of the agony of not belonging anywhere. My family and I experienced that firsthand. I would suppose there are multitudes of refugees in our world today and in the previous generation who went through that agony of not belonging, having no permanent place of their own.

These people in Hebrews 11 were seeking a place of their own, but not in this world. It says that if they had been interested and wanted, they could have gone back to the place they came from. Abraham, for instance, could have returned to Ur of the Chaldees. But he had his mind set forward, not backward. "They desired a better country, that is, a heavenly one."

Then comes this beautiful sentence: "Therefore God is not ashamed to be called their God." When we identify ourselves with God—His city and His preparation for us—then He is proud to be our God. It is beautiful to know that He has prepared a city—for them and for us.

Commitment to Jesus requires identification with His cross. We have to go out to Him to the place where He was crucified. This commitment to Him rules out two pursuits in our lives: pleasing self and pleasing the world.

Rule Out Pleasing Yourself

Let's look for a moment at what the New Testament says against pleasing self. Here are words from the apostle Paul:

> Brethren, join in following my example, and observe those who walk according to the pattern you have in us. For many walk, of whom I often told you, and now tell you even weeping, that they are enemies of the cross of Christ, whose end is destruction, whose God is their appetite, and whose glory is in their shame, who set their minds on earthly things.

Philippians 3:17–19

In this passage, it is clear to me that Paul is speaking about people who profess to be Christians—yet he warns his fellow believers against them. He says, "They claim to be followers of Christ, but they are the enemies of His cross. They are indulging self. Their minds are set on the things of this world. The principle of the cross—of death to self and the things of the flesh—has never been applied in their lives."

Regarding them, Paul says, "Be careful. Don't follow their example, because their end is destruction." It pains me to say it, but I think we have today people in the Church who profess allegiance to Christ—yet reject His cross.

Rule Out Pleasing the World

Our identification with the cross of Jesus also rules out pleasing this world. James writes these stern words in his epistle to professing believers: "You adulterous people, don't you know that friendship with the world is hatred toward God? Anyone who chooses to be a friend of the world becomes an enemy of God" (James 4:4 NIV1984).

This is very plain language—too plain for some people, I believe. Why does James call such people "adulterous"? Because, you see, the spiritual commitment to Jesus Christ required of us qualifies us to become part of His Bride. The Bride is required to have a single-hearted, total commitment and devotion to Jesus. If that commitment and devotion is infiltrated and adulterated by the love of this world, then we have become spiritual adulterers. We are not faithful to the Bridegroom, Jesus Christ. To be friendly with the world is to become spiritually adulterous.

We see this same thought in the words of Jesus:

"If the world hates you, keep in mind that it hated me first.
If you belonged to the world, it would love you as its own.
As it is, you do not belong to the world, but I have chosen
you out of the world. That is why the world hates you."

John 15:18–19 NIV1984

When the world "loves us as its own," that is a pretty dangerous sign that we do not belong to Jesus. Once again, this is plain language, and we need to give heed to it.

Only in the Cross

What then should be our attitude in the light of these plain facts and statements of Scripture? It is expressed in the words of Paul: "But may it never be that I should boast, except in the cross of our Lord Jesus Christ, through which the world has been crucified to me, and I to the world" (Galatians 6:14).

Those words make a deep impression on me. Let me never boast. Let me never place confidence in anything, ultimately, but the cross of the Lord. Let me not boast in my education, my religion, my denomination—none of these things. My only safe boast is in the cross of the Lord Jesus Christ, where Jesus won a total, permanent, irreversible victory over all the forces of evil. Through that cross, the world is crucified to me, and I to the world.

The cross is an absolute mark of separation between the people of God and the people of the world. When we accept the principle of the cross in our lives, we no longer belong to this world.

Jesus gives us this beautiful promise of victory: "I have told you these things, so that in me you may have peace. In this world you will have trouble. But take heart! I have overcome the world" (John 16:33 NIV1984).

That is good news, is it not? The world is not our friend—it is our enemy. We are going to have trouble, but Jesus has overcome the world! Through Jesus, we, too, can overcome the world—if we are willing to go out to Him, outside the camp, bearing His reproach. So, let us go out to Him.

14

Let Us Offer Up
a Sacrifice of Praise

I TRUST THAT you are finding in each of these chapters a growing sense of strength and direction as you set out to apply them personally. Remember that each step or resolution determines attitude, attitude determines approach, and approach determines outcome. In our next chapter, which is the final chapter of the book, we will look once more at all twelve resolutions for purposes of memorization.

1. Let us fear
2. Let us be diligent
3. Let us hold fast our confession
4. Let us draw near to the throne of grace
5. Let us press on to maturity
6. Let us draw near to the Most Holy Place
7. Let us hold fast our confession without wavering
8. Let us consider one another
9. Let us run with endurance the race
10. Let us show gratitude
11. Let us go out to Him

In this chapter, we will cover the twelfth and the final key found in the book of Hebrews.

KEY #12

"Let us offer up a sacrifice of praise"

Through Him [Jesus] then, let us continually offer up a sacrifice of praise to God, that is, the fruit of lips that give thanks to His name.

Hebrews 13:15

To me, this final key is very appropriate for the successful life, and it is very beautiful: "Let us continually offer up a sacrifice of praise to God." The final key is that which we are going to go on doing. Are you willing to go on doing what this verse says—continually offering up a sacrifice of praise to God? It will make all the difference in what the future holds for you.

Gratitude Leads to Praise

This final key, offering up a sacrifice of praise to God, is related in a direct and practical way to the two previous keys. Those are, "Let us show gratitude" and "Let us go out to Him outside the gate." Do you see the progression? Gratitude naturally leads to praise.

There are many passages in the Bible where thanksgiving is connected closely with praise. One of the most beautiful is Psalm 100:4: "[We] enter into His gates with thanksgiving, and into His courts with praise" (NKJV). The first step in access to God is thanksgiving; the second step is praise. Thanksgiving leads to praise. It finds expression in praise. It flows out in praise.

The key just before this one, "Let us go out to Him outside the camp," requires us to be identified with the cross of Jesus. To follow Jesus we must accept the reproach of His cross. As we pointed out, such an identification brings us release from the two slaveries of pleasing self and pleasing the world. This key is directly related to offering the sacrifice of praise. You might not see it at first, but the two hindrances to spontaneous, free-flowing praise in our lives are love of self and love of the world. As long as our affections are centered in ourselves or in the world, we are not really free to praise God. But the cross removes these two hindrances and sets us free to praise Him.

The Mystery of Liberty

When we experience the power of the cross in this liberating way, we are no longer affected by what happens to us. We are not affected by our moods, our problems or by apparent adversity. We are no longer affected by what goes on in the world around us.

At times, we might sit and listen to the news, and afterward think, "The situation is pretty bad. There are problems, disasters, crime, immorality. . . ." But you see, we are not living in this world. The world does not dominate us. It does not dominate our thinking. We are in the world but not of the world. Then, when we are released from that slavery to the world, when the world no longer controls our thinking and our motivations, when we have been liberated by the cross in that inner attitude toward the world, there is nothing left to hinder our praise. At that point, we do not praise God just when all is going right with the world. We do not praise God just when all is going right with ourselves. Rather, we praise God because He is worthy to be praised. Our liberated spirits are not entangled with self-love and the love of the world.

There is a tremendous mystery regarding the liberty that comes through being identified with the cross of Jesus. Praise is a significant aspect of that mystery. You can find out a lot about people when you study how much praising they do. You find out what kind of lives they are living. Are they still slaves of the "old man," or have they entered into the resurrected life of the "new man"?

The old man is a grumbler. When you hear a person grumbling, you know that is the old man speaking. But the new man is a praiser. So which are you? Is it the old man who speaks through you, or the new man who praises through you? The old man says, "I can't take this any longer. Things are getting too bad. Nobody treats me right. I don't know what's wrong with the world." The new man says, "Hallelujah! Praise the Lord! I'm free. I'm a child of God. Heaven is my home. God loves me." Which is your attitude?

In chapter 5, I quoted a sentence from Proverbs 18:21: "Death and life are in the power of the tongue, and those who love it will eat its fruit." There are two results that come out of the tongue: death and life. If you grumble, if you are negative or self-centered, your tongue will bring forth death. If you are liberated from all that, walking in the praise of God and the worship of God, your tongue will bring forth life. Please bear this in mind: Whatever your tongue brings forth in the way of fruit—whether sweet or bitter—you are going to eat that fruit.

Praise—A Sacrifice

I want to go back for a moment to that verse in Hebrews 13:15 and bring out one more important point. The writer says: "Through Him [Jesus] then, let us continually offer up a sacrifice of praise to God." One significant word there is *sacrifice*. Praise is a sacrifice. A sacrifice, according to the principles of Scripture, requires a death. Nothing was ever offered to God that had not passed through death. So we see from this insight that the sacrifice of praise requires the death of the old man.

The old man cannot really praise God as God deserves to be praised. There has to be a death. Then, too, a sacrifice costs something, and praise is costly. Let me put it this way: We need to praise God most when we least feel like it. Praise cannot depend on our feelings. It is a sacrifice of our spirits.

David's Example

David gives us a wonderful example of this. The introduction to Psalm 34 says, "A psalm of David when he feigned madness before Abimelech, who drove him away and he departed." At the time this psalm was written, David was a fugitive from his own country. King Saul was trying to kill him. David had to leave his familiar surroundings and was forced to seek refuge in the court of a Gentile king.

All the while, Abimelech the king suspected him of being an enemy. In order to save his own life, David had to feign madness. It says in the historical book that he scribbled on the door and he slobbered on his beard. That was his situation.

What was David's reaction to this desperate situation? We read it in the first three verses of this psalm:

> I will bless the LORD at all times; His praise shall continually be in my mouth. My soul shall make its boast in the LORD; the humble shall hear it and rejoice. O magnify the LORD with me, and let us exalt His name together.
>
> Psalm 34:1–3

Is that not marvelous? Right there, in such a terrible situation, with his life hanging in the balance and the shame of having to feign madness, David said, "I will bless the LORD at all times; His praise shall continually be in my mouth." That, my friend, is the sacrifice of praise. David's overriding desire was to go on boasting in the Lord. There may be nothing else for us to boast in, but we can boast in the Lord.

This psalm also says, "The humble will hear it and rejoice," followed by, "Let us exalt His name together."

Praise is infectious. But grumbling is infectious, too. If you grumble, you will get fellow grumblers. But when we learn to praise God this way, others will join us. Can we learn to offer that sacrifice of praise to God continually? If so, we will be obedient to our twelfth step toward a successful life: "Let us offer up a sacrifice of praise."

15

Successful Living

IN THIS CLOSING CHAPTER, I am going to review all the twelve keys we have looked at together through the course of this book. In addition, I will sum up the main lessons we have learned from each of them.

Review is an essential part of all successful teaching. I believe the review I am bringing to you here will help to imprint these keys on your mind. It will help to make them a real part of your life from now on. They have the potential to make your future years successful and blessed.

Key #1: Let Us Fear

> Therefore, let us fear lest, while a promise remains of entering His rest, any one of you should seem to have come short of it.
>
> Hebrews 4:1

This is the attitude of reverent respect for God and His requirements. Let me be clear: This is not a slavish fear—God has not given us a spirit of slavish fear. Instead, this is an attitude of reverence and respect for God, the opposite of self-confidence and presumptuousness. In order to walk in reverent respect and honor to the Lord, you and I must not only fear Him, but also lay aside any and all self-confidence and presumption.

Key #2: Let Us Be Diligent

> Let us therefore be diligent to enter that rest, lest anyone fall through following the same example of disobedience.
>
> Hebrews 4:11

"Let us fear" leads us on to "Let us be diligent." Not only should we not be presumptuous or self-confident—also we must not be negligent, but rather take life and commitment to the Lord seriously. As it were, we are to roll up our spiritual sleeves and go to work.

Connected to this key are two verses from Proverbs 10: "The blessing of the LORD . . . makes rich" (verse 22) and "The hand of the diligent makes rich" (verse 4). We put these two principles together to experience the blessing of the Lord. On one hand, it is His blessing; but on the other hand, it is our diligence that receives His blessing.

Key #3: Let Us Hold Fast Our Confession

> Since then we have a great high priest who has passed through the heavens, Jesus the Son of God, let us hold fast our confession.
>
> Hebrews 4:14

It is our confession that relates us to Jesus as our High Priest. We must make the right declaration with our mouths, making the words of our mouths agree with God's written Word. Every time we make the right confession, speaking it boldly in faith, Jesus is obligated by His eternal faithfulness to make sure our confessions are fulfilled. He is the High Priest of our confessions. We make a confession and then hold it fast in faith and perseverance.

Key #4: Let Us Draw Near to the Throne of Grace

> Let us therefore draw near with confidence to the throne of grace, that we may receive mercy and find grace to help in time of need.
>
> Hebrews 4:16

We are to come to the throne where Jesus sits as King— King of the universe, with all authority and power. He wants to help us, but we are obliged to be humble and acknowledge our need of help. This passage directs us to come for mercy and for grace, not for justice. Not for a due reward for our merits, but because we need Him. We come because He is faithful and because He invites us. We can come with confidence, therefore, even in the time of need, even when the situation is desperate. Even when we think there is no source of help, we can find help if we come to that throne of grace.

Key #5: Let Us Press On to Maturity

Therefore leaving the elementary teaching about the Christ,
let us press on to maturity.

Hebrews 6:1

We must move forward rather than remaining static in the Christian life. The Christian life is not a place to sit—it is a path to move along. "The path of the righteous is like the light of dawn, that shines brighter and brighter until the full day" (Proverbs 4:18). Therefore, as those who are in that way of righteousness and faith, we must be moving forward. Our goal is maturity—to be fully grown up, complete individuals in Christ. In that context, the only alternative to obedience is a sad one. What is that alternative?

The condition of arrested development, remaining forever spiritual infants, always tossed to and fro, never stable, never mature. The best alternative for you and me is that we press on together.

Key #6: Let Us Draw Near to the Most Holy Place

> Therefore, brothers, since we have confidence to enter the Most Holy Place by the blood of Jesus . . . let us draw near to God with a sincere heart.
>
> Hebrews 10:19, 22 niv1984

Putting together verses 19 and 22, "Let us draw near" in this context is "Let us draw near to the Most Holy Place." In an earlier resolution (Key #4), we were exhorted to draw near to the throne of grace. That was our invitation to come for help. But with Key #6, we are invited to go right in to the Most Holy Place—the place of God's own immediate presence, the place where God sits on the throne. We are invited to share the throne with Him.

Jesus is the forerunner who has gone before us. He is the new and living way. He died, was buried, rose again and was raised up into the glory of the Father. As we are identified with Him in each of those successive experiences—death, burial, resurrection and ascension into glory—we find that we have come into the Most Holy Place. We are entitled to draw near to that Most Holy Place and to enter in. This Scripture exhorts us to do so.

Key #7: Let Us Hold Fast Our Confession without Wavering

> Let us hold fast the confession of our hope without wavering, for He who promised is faithful.
>
> Hebrews 10:23

This key, of course, goes closely together with Key #3: "Let us hold fast our confession." Two very important words, however, are added: "Let us hold fast our confession *without wavering*." Why is it important that *without wavering* is put in? Circumstances will come along that could make us inclined to waver. There will be times of extreme pressure. There will be times of darkness—when everything seems to have gone wrong and it seems nothing is working out. What are we going to do then? Are we going to quit? Or are we going to hold fast without wavering? You and I must make up our minds right now that the next time the pressures come, we will not be quitters. We will hold fast without wavering—because He is faithful who promised. We might not see Him; we might not feel Him; He might seem to be far from the scene. But He is still there and He is still faithful.

Key #8: Let Us Consider One Another

> Let us consider how to stimulate one another to love and good deeds.
>
> Hebrews 10:24

Let us consider one another—this is our release from self-centeredness. Self-centered people are never happy people. They are never fully content. It always seems that something is missing from their lives, even though they may have everything the world has to offer. We can never find true peace and true inner rest as long as we are centered in ourselves. One practical remedy is to consider one another, to invest our lives in others, to provoke others to love and good deeds. I think one of the most applicable Scriptures for this key is Galatians 5:13: "Through love, serve one another." Put others first. Be more interested in them. We will get a wonderful response from them and, at the same time, we will get release from our own self-centeredness.

Key #9: Let Us Run with Endurance the Race

> Therefore, since we have so great a cloud of witnesses surrounding us, let us also lay aside every encumbrance, and the sin which so easily entangles us, and let us run with endurance the race that is set before us.
>
> Hebrews 12:1

The Christian life is like a race. There is a course marked out ahead of us. We have a goal, and there is a prize waiting. But if we are going to achieve the goal, if we are going to win the prize, we must run the race with the right attitude. We have to run it with endurance. We have to hold out. And to do that, we have to go into training.

Key #10: Let Us Show Gratitude

> Therefore, since we receive a kingdom which cannot be shaken, let us show gratitude, by which we may offer to God an acceptable service with reverence and awe.

Hebrews 12:28

There is a clear, close relationship between gratitude and grace. Having grace will always be expressed in being thankful. God expects us to appreciate what He does and to express our appreciation verbally.

Key #11: Let Us Go Out to Him

> Therefore Jesus also, that He might sanctify the people through His own blood, suffered outside the gate. Hence, let us go out to Him outside the camp, bearing His reproach.

Hebrews 13:12–13

This means that we identify ourselves not just with Jesus, but also with His cross. This means we are willing to recognize that this world is not our home, and that there is always a price to pay to be a Christian. We cannot lead the Christian life and reject the principles of the cross. The cross means death to self and death to the world.

Key #12: Let Us Offer Up a Sacrifice of Praise

> Through Him then, let us continually offer up a sacrifice of praise to God.
>
> Hebrews 13:15

Praise is the natural outcome of the previous eleven keys. It also sets the seal upon them and makes them sure.

Are You Ready?

There you have it—twelve intentional keys you can take hold of not only for a better year but for a better life. It is probably somewhat obvious to you that these resolutions that we have outlined are as challenging as they are life-changing. In fact, you cannot put them into practice without significant help from the Lord. It will take His abundant grace to accomplish everything you have read in this book. The good news is that His grace is there for the asking.

Having read this book, and being convinced of the truths therein, are you ready to ask the Lord to help you put it into practice? You can do so right now by praying the following prayer:

Dear Lord, I want to and need to take up the keys outlined in this book. I believe and proclaim that Your truth has the power through these principles to change my life permanently for the better.

I come to You now in the name of Jesus, asking for Your mercy and grace to help me in my time of need.

As sincerely as I know how at this moment, I commit myself fully to You and to the process of using these twelve keys to successful living.

I place myself and all aspects of my life in Your capable hands. Help me, Lord Jesus, by Your Holy Spirit, to fulfill the demands and requirements involved in using these keys.

For every good result and blessing that comes through Your grace and my obedience to You, I will be careful to give You all the praise, thanks, honor and glory. You alone deserve it, Lord Jesus—for it is in Your name that I pray. Amen.

General Index

Scripture Index

Derek Prince (1915–2003) was born in India of British parents. Educated as a scholar of Greek and Latin at Eton College and Cambridge University, England, he held a Fellowship in Ancient and Modern Philosophy at King's College. He also studied several modern languages, including Hebrew and Aramaic, at Cambridge University and the Hebrew University in Jerusalem.

While serving with the British army in World War II, he began to study the Bible and experienced a life-changing encounter with Jesus Christ. Out of this encounter he formed two conclusions: first, that Jesus Christ is alive; second, that the Bible is a true, relevant, up-to-date book. These conclusions altered the whole course of his life, which he then devoted to studying and teaching the Bible.

Derek's main gift of explaining the Bible and its teaching in a clear and simple way has helped build a foundation of faith in millions of lives. His nondenominational, nonsectarian approach has made his teaching equally relevant and helpful to people from all racial and religious backgrounds.

He is the author of more than 50 books, 600 audio and 110 video teachings, many of which have been translated and published in more than 100 languages. His daily radio broadcast is translated into Arabic, Chinese (Amoy, Cantonese, Mandarin, Shanghaiese, Swatow), Croatian, German, Malagasy, Mongolian, Russian, Samoan, Spanish and Tongan. The radio program continues to touch lives around the world.

Derek Prince Ministries persists in reaching out to believers in more than 140 countries with Derek's teachings, fulfilling the mandate to keep on "until Jesus returns." This is effected through the outreaches of more than 45 Derek Prince offices around the world, including primary work in Australia, Canada, China, France, Germany, the Netherlands, New Zealand, Norway, Russia, South Africa, Switzerland, the United Kingdom and the United States. For current information about these and other worldwide locations, visit www.derekprince.com.

More from Derek Prince

Do you sometimes feel trapped by a set of religious rules? Stop striving and walk away from the lies of legalism to experience the freeing power of His incredible grace.

By Grace Alone

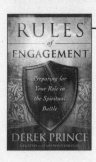

Discover how to build a warrior's character, face trials, fight alongside the Holy Spirit, influence the outcomes of spiritual battles and more!

Rules of Engagement

More from Derek Prince

Expose the forces at work behind the most common curses in your life so that you can experience freedom and blessing.

Blessing or Curse

Receive expert advice on how to remain free from demons and learn to recognize the fears and misconceptions often associated with their activities.

They Shall Expel Demons